Essential Teaching Principles:
A Resource Collection for Teachers

Compiled and Edited by Maryellen Weimer, PhD

Madison, Wisconsin

Magna Publications
2718 Dryden Drive
Madison, WI 53704
Magnapubs.com

Copyright © 2017 by Magna Publications.

The articles in this book have been previously published in *The Teaching Professor* newsletter, The Teaching Professor blog, or in the Faculty Focus blog.

ISBN: 978-0-912150-58-1

All rights reserved. Published 2017. It is unlawful to duplicate, transfer, or transmit this book in any manner without permission from the publisher.

Contents

Introduction 7
CHAPTER 1 • Effective Instruction Essentials 11
Introduction.. 12
  If you've never taught before
    What's in it for Me?.. 14
    Characteristics of Good Teachers... 17
  The case for active learning
    Active Learning Trumps Lecturing 19
    Practice Impacts Learning in a Large Physics Class 22
    Does Discussion Make a Difference? 24
  The syllabus (the motor that runs the course)
    The Course Syllabus: Contract, Culture, and Compass.... 26
    Can a Syllabus Cover Every Contingency? 29
  What to do when there's too much content to cover
    More Content Doesn't Equal More Learning 32
    Why Don't We Teach the Telephone Book? 35
  Assignments and grading policies shape learning experiences
    Thinking about Writing Assignments Developmentally ... 37
    Writing Good Assignment Descriptions 40
    Grading Policies and the Principles of Solid Measurement 43
  Taking your skills to the next level
    Introduction 45
  Teacher identity
    Six Myths about a Teaching Persona 47
  Improvement as an opportunity for learning
    Confessions of a Bad Teacher 50
    On Becoming a Teacher 53
    Sustaining Excellence 55
    "What Works" in the Messy Landscape of
    Teaching and Learning 57
    Why Are We So Slow to Change the Way We Teach?....... 60

CHAPTER 2 • Course Design Principles 63
When you've got a course to design or one to plan
Introduction 64
Backward Design, Forward Progress 65
PowerPoint: Key Considerations 69
Keeping courses fresh and effective
Introduction 72
A Course Redesign Improves Attitudes and Performance 73
Refresh Your Course without (Too Much) Pain and Suffering 76
Handouts that Encourage Active Participation 80

CHAPTER 3 • Students and Learning 83
Introduction 84
Missing basic skills
Note-Taking: A Helpful Handout for Students 85
Reading Prompts 87
Reading Groups Get Students Reading 90
Behaviors that compromise learning
Excuses, Excuses, Excuses 92
Cramming for Exams 94
Multitasking: It Doesn't Mix Well with Learning 96
Metacognitive Pestering for Beginning Students 98
A primer on learning
Introduction 100
Learning: Five Key Principles 101
Metacognition: Three Ways Students Can Learn about Learning ... 103
Understanding motivation
Introduction 106
Understanding Student Motivation 108
More and better participation
Reasons Why Students Do or Don't Participate 112
The Art of Asking Questions 114
Ways of Responding to a Wrong or Not Very Good Answer 117
Clickers: Taking a Look at the Research 119
Keys to successful group work
Designing Group Work 122
Improving Group Projects 124
Peer Assessment in Small Groups 127

CHAPTER 4 • Creating Climates for Learning..........................129
Introduction.. 130
What is a learning climate and how do you create it?
Classroom Climates 132
Factors that Lead to Rapport 134
Being present in class, online, and during office hours
Witness the Struggle: The Gifts of Presence, Silence, and Choice ... 136
Who and what needs to be managed?
Why Policies Fail to Promote Better Learning Decisions 139

CHAPTER 5 • Teaching Online..143
Introduction.. 144
Never taught online before?
Top 10 Rules for Developing Your First Online Course 145
Five Factors that Affect Online Student Motivation 148
Tips for Building Social Presence in Your Online Class 151
Discussion that's more than posting comments
Art and Science of Successful Online Discussions 154
Online Discussion Questions That Work....................................... 158
Evaluating Online Discussions.. 161

CHAPTER 6 • Quizzes, Exams, and Finals:
Assessment that Promotes Learning 163
Introduction.. 164
Quizzes
Quizzes That Deepen Engagement with Course Content 166
Exams and finals
Test Review Sessions: A Better Design... 169
Cumulative Exams.. 172
Helping Students Prepare for Cumulative Exams 174
Final Fitness and the Louisiana 2-Step.. 177
Reasons for extra credit, dropping low scores,
or makeup exams
Make-Up Exams... 180
Revisiting Extra Credit Policies... 183
Prevent cheating or promote academic integrity?
Cheating: Are We Part of the Problem? 186

CHAPTER 7 • Feedback and Grading 189
Introduction 190
Feedback from the teacher, peers, and self
Making Teacher Feedback Useful 193
Peer Review: Successful from the Start 196
Developing Students' Self-Assessment Skills: Is It Possible? 199
Making grading a manageable task
Grading Advice for When There's Lots to Grade
and Not a Lot of Time 202
Rubrics: Worth Using? 204
Grading policies and practices that make grades more about learning
Using Grading Policies to Promote Learning 207
When the student objects to the grade
The "I Deserve a Better Grade on This" Conversation 210

CHAPTER 8 • Feedback for Teachers 213
Introduction 214
What can I learn about my teaching?
Writing to Reflect and Improve 216
Can You Write Your Way to Better Teaching? 218
What can I learn from students?
Negative Student Comments on Course Ratings 221
Sharing the Feedback 224
What can I learn from others?
Becoming a Better Teacher: Articles for New and
Not-So-New Faculty 226
What We Learn from Each Other 230

Additional Resources 233

Introduction

What is this?

It's a collection of resources on teaching and learning—it's not a book. It does have chapters, but each chapter contains a collection of short readings on a topic. The chapter opens with an introduction that highlights key aspects of what's covered by the resources.

Who's the collection for?

It's been assembled for those who are teaching college-level curriculum in high school. I'm leaving it up to you to decide whether this collection might support your attempts to master instructional details and teach in ways that support learning. It's a collection for those who believe (or at least suspect) there are many things about college-level teaching and learning that could profitably be learned. And it's been put together by someone who thinks that what needs to be learned about teaching and learning is interesting beyond belief and can be mastered, although not always as easily or quickly as many new teachers think. Good teaching is not a gift; it's not something you're born knowing how to do. It's the result of a carefully honed set of skills.

It's a collection that's relevant no matter what you teach. Yes, there are aspects of teaching unique to the content you teach, and those are best learned from colleagues in the field. But there are also significant parts of teaching and learning that transcend disciplines. Much of what teachers need to know can be learned from others, including those who teach in dissimilar fields.

What's in the collection?

As for the resources themselves, they include short (700 to 1,000 words) pieces reprinted from various Magna publications. Some of these articles offer advice, and others describe good practices. Some propose techniques, activities, strategies, or policies. Some aspire to make you think and to challenge assumptions frequently held by new teachers, and others highlight interesting research findings. There are also short quotations, facts, and data bits that are simply described as "something to think about".

And there are references, but not a lot. There could be a lot. Scholarship on teaching and learning is being published in every discipline as well as in the fields that officially study it. But teaching can be pretty overwhelming on any number of fronts. Class sessions are scheduled, and it's your responsibility to be present and prepared. You may be teaching content you've never taught before. You may be teaching multiple courses, and some of them to a large number of students. So how much time do you have to devote to materials on how to teach? With that in mind, I've selected a few really outstanding resources, books, and articles that strengthen the foundation that this collection begins to build. If you don't have time to get to them now, circle and star. They'll be there, and I think you'll be glad you found your way to them.

What's in the collection can also mean what topics are covered. You can see those in the table of contents. It's an interesting question, or at least it was for me when I was deciding what materials to include. Of all that could be shared with new teachers, what's essential? What are the first things they need to know? What aspects of teaching matter most when the goal is helping students learn?

This collection is only an introduction. My hope is that it's intriguing enough that this initial encounter will motivate you to read and discover more about teaching and learning. As with so many things we study, there's always more to learn.

What makes this collection unique?

It's not a prescriptive book, intended to give advice. There's not one right way to do any aspect of teaching. In some senses, teachers have to find their own way. Advice helps, but given the complexity of teaching, the variety of contexts in which it occurs, the many kinds of content being taught, and the proclivities of individual teachers, it's tough to come up with advice that fits every instructional situation and teacher.

The content also makes it unique. The other kind of instructional material most often given to teachers is techniques—the nuts, bolts, and how-tos of teaching. And those are needed. You're never going to teach well without good techniques, but are they what should be learned first?

Some, maybe, and there are a number in this collection, but they aren't the main focus. There's so much more to teaching than techniques, and those "how-to" details are not what make teaching challenging or satisfying. What's more important early on, I believe, is developing constructive ways of thinking about teaching and learning—methods that set you up for continued growth, ways that help you deal with mistakes and failure, and ways to think about students and the vexing challenges presented by today's diverse and not always well-prepared college populations.

What is the best way to use the collection?

Ultimately you'll decide what works best for you, but here are some ways you might consider.

You can simply cruise through the collection. Before each of the longer pieces, I've included a "Reason to read," which essentially is the reason I selected it for the collection. If something looks good, you can read it; if it doesn't, skip it. This approach probably works best for those who have time only to sit down and look through the collection.

You can look for an area you need help with: grading, assignment design, getting students to participate, quizzing strategies, classroom management. Don't go overboard here. You may feel you need help with everything, which probably isn't the case. Figure out what's most pressing and find resources that address the areas where you most need guidance. To expedite finding what you most need to know, I've included a list of issues and questions that frequently perplex teachers and the relevant items in the collection.

You can proceed through the collection chapter by chapter, although they don't have to be read in the order they appear. It does make sense to start at the beginning if you're a brand-new teacher, but after that or if you aren't brand-new, you can go to whatever chapter strikes your fancy. Many of the materials in the collection really beg to be discussed. They're provocative. You probably won't agree with everything. Material like that becomes even more meaningful when you talk about it with someone else. It can be someone who teaches the same content as you or someone who teaches in another field. But share something from this collection (you don't have to feel guilty—these aren't 15-page articles) and then talk about your thoughts and reactions.

And finally a word of welcome to this collection and, more important, to college level teaching. There aren't words to describe how much I love teaching and how committed I am to helping teachers learn about this intensely satisfying work. Teaching changes people's lives—those who teach and those who learn. It matters in ways large and small. I can't think of a better way to spend a life.

Maryellen Weimer, PhD
Editor, *The Teaching Professor*
Author, the Teaching Professor Blog

CHAPTER 1

•

Effective Instruction Essentials

Introduction

Teaching is one of those tasks where it's hard to know where to start, especially if you've never done it before. It's easy to get overwhelmed.

In the beginning it's best to focus on the essentials—the most important parts of teaching and learning. There will be lots of other things that you could (and perhaps should) be doing, but for your first few times in the college classroom, work on the basics. And what might those be? Well, there isn't a definitive list that everybody agrees on, but the topics covered in this section would end up on lots of those lists.

You'll get the most out of your first teaching experiences if you begin with a healthy, realistic perspective on teaching. Most of us come to teaching for the right reasons. We have great expectations for our students and ourselves. Most of us find our early teaching experiences both exciting and disappointing. It helps to begin by recognizing you won't do it all right the first (second, third, or any) time. First teaching experiences are great learning opportunities, and what you learn can make you a better teacher.

It's hard to underestimate the importance of the role teachers play in students' learning. The decisions you make about content determine what students learn—that's pretty obvious. Your decisions about assignments, testing strategies, and grading policies determine how students will learn. But students learn things other than simply content in courses. Whether or not teachers like it, they are role models. Students look at teachers and see professionals in action. They also look at teachers and see people. Sometimes they connect with a teacher and powerful learning results.

The case for active learning. It's a convincing one. We learn best by doing. We can watch somebody engaged in problem solving and learn a few things from that observation. But we really learn how to solve problems by solving them ourselves. This is exactly what most of us have discovered about learning to teach. You can get good background information (that's what a collection like this aspires to provide) and it will be helpful. There are things about teaching you can learn by reading and things you can learn from others, but the real learning occurs when you start teaching. The principle is simple, but we've had centuries of teachers telling students what they need to know without providing nearly enough opportunities for practice.

What makes the case particularly convincing at this time is an abundance of recent research that compares learning outcomes when teachers rely on lecture and when they use of active learning strategies. The resources offer a summary of this research and some specific examples. There's no need to abandon lecture; teaching as telling has its place. But in most courses, the place it occupies should be significantly smaller.

The syllabus—use it to run the course. Course logistics matter—first time out, use the syllabus as your course planning document and let it become what guides you through the course. You can think of it as a map. Since you're new in the territory, a detailed map will keep you from getting lost, and good directions make the destination much easier to find.

But the syllabus communicates more than just course logistics. It says something about who you are, how you feel about the content, and what you think about students. The tone of the syllabus matters. Try to think more about issuing an invitation to learning and less about creating a set of rules and regulations that establish who's in charge.

The content—what to do when there's too much to cover. In almost every course, there is too much content to cover. Our thoughts about content need to change. The goal should not be covering (are we talking about concealing?) the content, but using it to develop content knowledge and learning skills. We have passed the point where we can teach students everything they need to know about anything. We need to be using the content to develop skills that support lifelong learning.

But for many new to teaching, or new to a department or institution, the decision to cut content should not be made lightly. Reputations (of courses and of teachers) are often linked to the rigor of a course, and hard courses are filled with lots of complicated content. But teaching efficiently, holding students responsible for learning some of the content on their own, and better integrating content and process can help faculty manage what students are expected to learn in a course.

Assignments and grading policies shape learning experiences. They set the parameters within which learning occurs. They create the conditions under which learning occurs. And students are not the ones who set these parameters and/or create these conditions.

Too often with assignments and grading policies, teachers do as other teachers do, or do what they think they're expected to do. It's fine to acquaint yourself with what's customary for the course or in the department, but decisions about assignments and grading policies should be yours.

If you've never taught before

What's in it for Me?

Reason to read: You want to be teaching for the right reasons. Yes, there are pragmatic reasons: You have to make a living. But if that's the only reason, then it's a bit like asking students what they want to get out of a course and having them say "a good grade." Teaching can be about a lot more than the paycheck (thank goodness, given the size of most teacher paychecks) and here's a list of those rewards.

These days, when the focus is on students and learning, it may not seem appropriate for teachers to be asking, "What's in it for me?" Facilitating student learning is not without benefits, but what else is there in the college teaching profession for us? William Buskist has compiled a list of 10 rewards that come to those who teach. Here's a brief description of each.

Enjoying the intellectual challenge. "Teaching is through and through an intellectual endeavor, especially if it is to be done well." (p. 35) It is about communicating content we love, having a reason to keep current and an excuse to explore and re-explore areas that we find fascinating. We get paid to talk about ideas that capture our imaginations.

Enjoying solving "engineering problems." "Knowing the content is one thing; engineering the optimum learning environment…is something entirely different." (p. 35) It's about assembling a complicated puzzle that includes what to teach, how to present it, what resources to use to support it, what assignment features expedite learning, how to assess that learning, and how to establish rapport and motivate students. And if you get it figured out for one class, great—but expect the same challenge in the next course when the dynamics have changed and what worked before may not now.

Acquiring and refining communication skills. "A person with a brain full of knowledge is not a teacher…until he or she can convey that knowledge to another person." (p. 36) Teaching provides opportunities to develop sophisticated communication skills, many of which are transferable to other venues, like department meetings, conference presentations, and interviews.

Sharing our passion. We get to share what we love, regularly. We get to talk about why psychology, geology, math, or business logistics just happens to be the best discipline in the whole world. Sometimes our passion ignites a similar love in students. They major in the field, go on to make great contributions, and along the way, give us credit for their presence in the discipline.

Making a difference in students' lives. Buskist reports that he asked a small group of psychology students (about 20) what it meant to have teachers make a difference in their lives "and not one of them reported 'learning psychology.'" (p. 36) No, almost three-quarters said that teachers made a difference in their lives by helping them "discover their academic and personal strengths," by helping them believe more in themselves. There is great satisfaction to be had in knowing that you've changed some students' lives for the better.

Recruiting the next generation of psychologists. Buskist is a psychologist, so that's the field to which he wants students recruited. He writes about the satisfaction that comes from knowing that you're helping the discipline to move forward, helping ensure that the brain power needed to continue to advance knowledge in the field will be there. "In a very real sense, watching our students succeed in this way validates our work as teachers and inspires us to continue it." (p. 37)

Delighting in self-discovery. "Teaching, especially reflective teaching, can be a powerful catalyst for our personal development as human beings." (p. 37) Through teaching, we learn important things about ourselves. We can look back and see how we've grown and changed. Teaching expresses personhood, thereby giving us the chance to encounter who we are and what we believe.

Enjoying the fun that teaching is. It certainly is not one of those jobs where you know exactly what's going to happen and when. Each day in class is a whole new adventure, and when the class goes well, when you can feel the energy and excitement that comes with learning, it's just plain fun.

Enjoying the good company of other teachers. Buskist quotes an exemplary psychology teacher, Bill Hill, who captures this essence of this reward: "I think the friendships and experiences around teaching and colleagues are the best part of an academic life, or for that matter, any line of work." (p. 38)

Enjoying being a good teacher. "Teachers take pride in doing their jobs well." (p. 38) It's a profession where the work is important, where it matters, and where doing it has its own rewards. We've all had those days, those courses, those years when we really and truly love what we do.

Reference: Buskist, W. (2008). Teaching: What's in it for Me? *Essays from Excellence in Teaching*, 8 (9), 35–39. Electronic resource found at www.teachpsych.org/resources

---

Reprinted from *The Teaching Professor,* Feb 2010

Recommended Resource

McKeachie, W. and Svinicki, M. D. *Teaching Tips: Strategies, Research and Theory for College and University Teachers.* 14th ed., Belmont, CA: Wadsworth, 2014.

There's a good chance this book on teaching and learning been read by more college teachers than any other book on the subject. It's a classic—an if-you-can-only-take-one-book kind of classic. Every edition since the first, published in the late 1930s, authored by Bill McKeachie, is thoroughly updated so the book remains current. It's well organized, easy to read, and offers sound advice, virtually all of it research-based. This book promoted evidence-based teaching long before it was trendy.

Characteristics of Good Teachers

Reason to read: The characteristics of good teaching have been listed, explored, studied, and explained since the early 1900s. What makes teachers effective isn't a secret—it isn't something you're "gifted" with at birth; it rests on attitudes you can cultivate and skills you can develop. This particular list focuses on teacher characteristics that promote learning.

- Good teachers are also good learners; for example, they learn through their own reading, by participating in a variety of professional development activities, by listening to their students, by sharing ideas with their colleagues, and by reflecting on classroom interactions and students' achievements. Good teaching is therefore dynamic, reflective, and constantly evolving.

- Good teachers display enthusiasm for their subject and a desire to share it with their students.

- Good teachers know how to modify their teaching strategies according to the particular students, subject matter, and learning environment.

- Good teachers encourage learning for understanding and are concerned with developing their students' critical-thinking skills, problem-solving skills, and problem-approach behaviors.

- Good teachers demonstrate an ability to transform and extend knowledge, rather than merely transmitting it; they draw on their knowledge of their subject, their knowledge of their learners, and their general pedagogical knowledge to transform the concepts of the discipline into terms that are understandable to their students.

- Good teachers set clear goals, use valid and appropriate assessment methods, and provide high-quality feedback to their students.

- Good teachers show respect for their students; they are interested in both their professional and their personal growth, encourage their independence, and sustain high expectations of them.

This description, provided by the authors below, sets the bar high. But it ably captures the essence of what teachers should aspire to be and do for students.

Reference: Ramsden, P. D., Margetson, E. M., and Clarke, S. *Recognizing and Rewarding Good Teaching.* Canberra: Australian Government Printing Services, 1995.

Reprinted from The Teaching Professor blog, Mar 2, 2010

Something to think about…
"Teaching is not about charismatically charged individuals using the sheer force of their characters and personalities to wreak lifelong transformations in students' lives. It's about finding ways to promote the day-to-day, incremental gains that students make as they try to understand ideas, grasp concepts, assimilate knowledge, and develop new skills. All the small things you do to make this happen for students represent the real story of teaching. Helping learning is what makes you truly heroic." (p. 276)

Reference: Brookfield, S. D. *The Skillful Teacher: On Technique, Trust, and Responsiveness in the Classroom.* 3rd ed. San Francisco: Jossey-Bass, 2015.

The case for active learning

Active Learning Trumps Lecturing

Reason to read: Here's the most comprehensive review of research comparing active learning and lecture published so far.

This meta-analysis of 225 studies compares STEM (Science, Technology, Engineering, and Math) classes taught using various active learning approaches with classes taught via lecture. "The results indicate that average examination scores improved by about 6 percent in active learning sessions, and that students in classes with traditional lecturing were 1.5 times more likely to fail than were students in classes with active learning." (p. 8410) Carl Wieman, a Nobel-winning physicist who now does research on teaching and learning, describes the work as a "massive effort" that provides "a much more extensive quantitative analysis of the research on active learning in college and university STEM courses than previously existed." (p. 8319) And what does he make of these results? "The implications of these meta-analysis results for instruction are profound, assuming they are indicative of what could be obtained if active learning methods replaced the lecture instruction that dominates U.S. postsecondary STEM instruction." (pp. 8319–8320) That's a long way from the guarded language usually found in commentaries on scientific results.

The findings of the meta-analysis aren't are all that unexpected. Study after study—not just in the STEM fields, but pretty much across the board—has reported findings that favor active learning approaches over lecture. Most of us know that learning is harder from the sidelines. If deep understanding is the objective, then the learner had best get out there and play the game. Watching others problem-solve, think critically, paint with watercolors, or start an IV may provide a sense of how it's done, but that's not how you learn to perform those tasks.

There is less defense of lecture than there used to be, and more apologizing by those who do. "I have to lecture. What else can you do in these large classes?" "I can't get the content covered if I don't lecture." "Students want me to lecture." Valid excuses? Not really. Examples of active learning strategies being used in large classes abound. Teachers may cover the content, but if this doesn't promote learning, does it really matter that it's been covered? And since when did education become governed by what learners may think they need or want?

But despite what we know, those apologies, and the resulting feelings of guilt, there's still an awful lot of lecture happening in most fields and on most campuses. It remains our default instructional mode. We go there first and we stay there the longest. Lecturing allows us to pledge allegiance to the content.

This may sound adamant, but the evidence is in. The case is closed. Active learning wins. If we aspire to make our practice evidence-based, then we need to conduct a very honest analysis of how often we find ourselves front and center, covering the content. We need to more aggressively raise the issue with our colleagues, in our departments, at our institutions, and within our professional associations.

No, lecturing doesn't need to be against the law, with harsh sentences levied against those who continue to do it. There are times when teachers need to share their expertise, when efficiency makes telling students the only reasonable option. Teachers can explain things clearly, cogently, and with passion. There's a place for that as well, but it's a much smaller place than it currently occupies in many classrooms.

It is true that we still don't know as much about active learning as we need to. For example, we don't how much is needed to make a difference in a class session or across the course. We don't know which of the many active learning approaches (group work, clickers, online discussion, hands-on experience, etc.) work best with what kinds of content and for what kinds of learners. We've got lots to learn, but we definitely know enough to challenge ourselves and our colleagues to step back from lecture and move forward with approaches that feature students taking action.

References:

Freeman, S., Eddy, S. L., McDonough, M., Smith, M. K., Okorafor, N., Jordt, H., and Wenderoth, M. P., (2014). Active learning increases student performance in science, engineering, and mathematics. *Proceedings of the National Academy of Sciences* (PNAS), 111 (23), 8410–8415.

Weiman, C. E., (2014. Large-scale comparison of science teaching methods sends clear message. *Proceedings of the National Academy of Sciences (PNAS)*, 111 (23), 8319–8320.

Reprinted from The Teaching Professor blog, Jun 3, 2015

Recommended Resource
Barkley, E. F. Student Engagement Techniques: A Handbook for College Faculty. San Francisco: Jossey-Bass, 2010.
So, you're thinking there ought to be more active learning activities in your courses, but you're short on ideas? Here's a super collection: 100 different strategies, each described in detail, illustrated with examples, and proposed in various formats.

Practice Impacts Learning in a Large Physics Class

Reason to read: It's good to start with the broad conclusions of a meta-analysis, but it's also persuasive to get into the specifics of an individual study, and here's a good example.

In this large physics class, practice took "the form of a series of challenging questions and tasks that require[d] students to practice physicist-like reasoning and problem-solving during class time while provided with frequent feedback." (p. 862)

The design of this particular study is interesting. It involved two large sections of a first-year physics course, one enrolling 267 students and the other 271 students. For the first 11 weeks of the course, both sections were taught similarly; they had different teachers, but the same content, same assignments, same labs, and same exams. During week 12, students in the experimental section used deliberate practice. They spent "all their time in class… 'thinking scientifically' in the form of making and testing predictions and arguments about the relevant topics, solving problems, and critiquing their own reasoning and that of others." (p. 862) Students in the control section listened to lectures on the same content.

A test which measured conceptual knowledge of the content covered during this experimental week was taken by students in both sections immediately after the week ended. Researchers also tracked attendance and student engagement during this week. Students did not receive credit for taking this exam. Even so, 171 in the control section and 211 in the experimental section took the test. Average scores were 41 percent in the control section and 74 percent in the experimental section. "Random guessing would produce a score of 23 percent, so the students in the experimental section did more than twice as well on this test as those in the control section." (p. 863) The test score distributions for the two sections showed little overlap, "demonstrating that the differences in learning between the two sections exist for essentially the entire population." (p. 864)

During the week of the experiment, attendance and engagement were unchanged in the control section, but in the experimental section, engagement nearly doubled and attendance increased by 20 percent.

Even though the experiment represented a significant change in how the class operated and was only used for one week, 90 percent of the students agreed or strongly agreed with this statement: "I really enjoyed the interactive teaching technique during the three lectures on E&M [electricity and magnetic] waves." Only 1 percent disagreed. Seventy-seven percent agreed with this statement: "I feel I would have learned more if the whole Physics 153 course would have been taught in this highly interactive style." (p. 864)

Reference: Deslauriers, L., Schelew, E., and Wieman, C. (2011). Improved learning in a large-enrollment physics class. Science, 332 (13 May), 862–865.

Revised version originally published in *The Teaching Professor,* Aug/Sep 2012

Does Discussion Make a Difference?

Reason to read: When students talk to each other about the content, does that kind of discussion improve learning?

Here's the scenario: Students are taking a chemical thermodynamics course. The instructor solicits clicker responses to a conceptually based multiple-choice question. Students answer individually, write a brief explanation in support of their answer, and indicate how confident they are that their answer is correct. They are then encouraged to discuss their answers with two or three (self-selected) other students. After that discussion, they have the opportunity to change their answer if they wish, write another explanation for the answer, and once again indicate their degree of confidence in their answer. Do you think that discussion would make a difference here—and, in particular, would it make a difference in their understanding of the concept?

That's the protocol students followed in the research referenced below. In one cohort, students saw how the rest of the class answered the question before they discussed; in a second cohort, they did not.

The results came down pretty substantially on the side of discussion. "A statistically significant number of students who originally had the correct multiple-choice answer had a higher value code assigned to their explanation after group discussion, and therefore demonstrated more explicit understanding of difficult concepts in chemical thermodynamics." (p. 1482) In other words, even though they had correctly answered the question before discussing it with peers, students had a richer understanding of the answer after such discussion. The same was true for students who initially answered the question incorrectly. Regardless of whether they corrected their answer or answered incorrectly again, in both cases, such students improved the code value of their explanations. Only when students changed a correct answer to an incorrect one did the code value of their explanation decline. However, the number of students who changed correct answers was small compared to the number who changed from incorrect to correct answers.

Whether or not students saw answer results before discussion did not seem make a difference in whether answers were changed or in the quality of the explanations offered for the answers. Confidence in the correctness of the answer was enhanced when students saw the class response and it agreed with their answer. Likewise, when they saw the answer chosen by the majority of the class and it was not the answer they selected, their confidence diminished.

Interestingly, in this study, students spent an average of seven minutes in discussion. Perhaps their interactions were richer because they not only answered the question, but had written an explanation supporting the answer they chose. Also of note, extra credit was awarded to students who answered correctly, which probably served to motivate participation in the discussion.

This research confirms findings reported in other studies. When faced with conceptual problems, students need the opportunity to practice solving them. That value of that practice is enhanced when, in addition to finding the answer, students talk to one another about the problem and how they arrived at their answers. What's most encouraging in this study is the documentation that such discussion not only leads more of them to the correct answer, it improves their ability to explain why the answer is correct.

Reference: Brooks, B. J., and Koretsky, M. D. (2011). The influence of group discussion on students' responses and confidence during peer instruction. *Journal of Chemical Education*, 88, 1477–1484.

Reprinted from *The Teaching Professor*, Apr 2013

Something to think about…

Although active learning results in better learning outcomes than straight lecture, most active learning converts don't abandon lecture. "Tired descriptors like 'sage-on-the-stage' and 'guide-on-the-side' have permeated the pedagogical literature for over two decades now, even though they greatly oversimplify what really takes place in the college classroom. Most teaching occurs on a continuum between these two extremes."

Reference: Cox, J. R., and Yearwood, D. (2013). In defense of teaching. *The Teaching Professor* (January).

The syllabus (the motor that runs the course)

The Course Syllabus: Contract, Culture, and Compass

by *Kiren Dosanjh Zucker, Lori Baker-Schena, and Mira Pak* — *California State University, Northridge*

Reason to read: The syllabus is a multi-faceted artifact of teaching. It can accomplish a variety of goals, many of them essential to a smooth-running course. This piece introduces three.

In the courses we teach, the syllabus serves several purposes. First, it represents a contract between instructor and students. Second, it helps to establish the culture of a class, whether the course is held online or in a traditional classroom. Third, it offers a compass to guide students toward achievement of the course's learning objectives.

ContractMake the elements of student success transparent. Articulate expectations, but do not "waive your discretion."

Like a contract, a syllabus both establishes and manages expectations for you and your students. Each expectation should be identified, defined, and communicated. Consequences for actions like submitting assignments late should be addressed, with room saved for discretion. A comprehensive, detailed syllabus eliminates the element of surprise that leads to student frustration, but it should not rid you of your power to make reasonable decisions. For example, using words and phrases such as "may" or "up to and including" in grading policies will allow you to apply standards sensibly.

The syllabus also establishes timelines. Weekly schedules that include required reading, assignments, quizzes, and tests support students' preparation. Starting each class session with a review of the week's schedule shifts students' focus to the task at hand, and offers the instructor another opportunity to manage expectations.

Present the syllabus as a contract during the first class session. Invest class time to carefully review it and ensure that students understand what is expected of them. Consider having students sign the syllabus to underscore the responsibilities it spells out for them. Offer students an incentive for thoroughly reviewing the course syllabus by giving a "syllabus quiz" early in the semester for bonus points on a future exam.

Culture

Create the kind of learning experience you want students to have.

In every course, the teacher and students form a learning community. The syllabus provides an opportunity to build a "classroom culture" by identifying core values, establishing norms, and explaining standards of conduct.

State the norms of conduct you expect students to follow in class. Consider including a "civility policy" that requires, for example, students to turn off cell phones in class and respect others' opinions. Describe the "core values" of the class and how they are reflected in the course's requirements and expectations (e.g. teamwork, respect, honesty, truth). Include an "academic honesty policy" that addresses such issues as plagiarism with clearly communicated rules and expectations, as well as the consequences for violation.

Consider what your syllabus explicitly or implicitly communicates about you as a teacher. For example, do you encourage students to email you questions or visit during your office hours? What classroom activities have you planned, and are they mentioned in the class schedule?

Through your syllabus, you are conducting an initial conversation with your students. Address the individual student in the syllabus. In describing expectations, use the second person: "You are expected to be prepared to participate in each class" versus "Students are expected to be prepared to participate in each class." Communicating directly with students in the syllabus underscores that they have the power and responsibility to meet course expectations. Put yourself in it. Using the first person rather than the third person (e.g. "I" instead of "the instructor") as you explain your office hours, availability, etc. subtly communicates your enthusiasm and commitment to students' learning—cornerstones of a healthy classroom culture.

Compass

Align your course requirements to student learning outcomes.

Before you leave on a trip, knowing your destination is essential to plotting out your route. The syllabus should provide a clear path to the end goal: the course's student learning outcomes. *Setting the learning outcomes first* keeps your students focused on the destination and helps you determine how to guide them there. Each activity, reading, assignment, and formative assessment should clearly assist students on their path toward the learning outcomes. Given the limited class time in a semester, assess each planned activity with this question: does it provide students with a learning experience that will move them closer to the expected learning outcome? If not, then you should consider eliminating that activity. If you choose to do the activity anyway, define its purpose, such as building community in class.

The summative assessment offered by the final exam allows students to show you how well they met the learning goals of the class. Formative assessments like regular quizzes help you determine whether the route to the goals might need to be reconsidered or changed. The summative exam is a roadmap of the course: can you trace back to specific activities, readings, and assignments in the course and see how they lead to the final destination? Formative activities keep you and the students on track and allow you both to monitor progress toward the learning goals.

Knowing where you want to end up allows you to plan how you will get there. This information is invaluable to both you and your students. Put it in your course syllabus and you'll be getting the semester off to a strong start.

Note: Parts of this article first appeared in a CSU Northridge blog, "Ideas for Faculty."

Reprinted from *The Teaching Professor,* Jan 2010

Can a Syllabus Cover Every Contingency?

by Rob Dornsife, Creighton University, Nebraska

Reason to read: It's possible to get carried away with policies in the syllabus. You simply can't regulate everything necessary for learning to happen. This piece offers a poignant illustration of what policies can't prevent.

I was recently asked by a friend and colleague to review her syllabus. She wanted to make sure she had enough policies to address all the classroom issues that emerge these days. Policies regarding plagiarism, class cancellation procedures, references to various official University Handbook codes, and even mandated contingencies for an H1N1 virus outbreak were dutifully laid out. Indeed, the syllabus, despite some mention of the course itself, read far more like a legal document than an introduction and guide to a classroom experience.

My colleague reported that this is what she had been told to include on the syllabus and she was anxious to do what was expected. Still, I sensed she was not totally comfortable with what her syllabus had become. For example, her section on the college's process for handling plagiarism was twice as long as her succinct description of what and how the students might be expected to engage with the actual course material, in this case, a terrific assignment sequence geared around eco-critical thinking, writing, and awareness.

As I listened to her struggle to explain and justify the various policies, I, gently and in good humor, began asking questions about the loopholes—the ones that in my experience, some students have keen ways of navigating to their perceived advantage. Was a roommate's grandmother's recurrent illness a "genuine emergency?" What constituted an "outbreak" of a virus? Were all students who appeared to have cheated to be treated identically and absolutely? It quickly became clear that while fair policies are desirable and necessary, no policy can address any and all eventualities and none are immune to student attempts at circumvention.

"So, what do we do?" my colleague asked. Even though I've struggled with these issues, I was a bit surprised by the first response that came to me.

"We need to remain vulnerable, and we need to celebrate our vulnerabilities as teachers."

Now that I've had bit of time to reflect, I've decided that it's a good response. If I am not willing to be vulnerable to my students, I am not able to teach them. There are risks here—and not just a few, and not just those associated with our policies and their loopholes. Being vulnerable is the inevitable result of the trust we must have in our students, as we expect to teach and learn from and with them in every respect.

I recently had a student who was missing classes and was not submitting work. In a supportive spirit, I invited him for a talk. I explained that I really wanted to help him pass the course. Surprised that his performance was in such peril, he replied that he needed to pass the course; he was graduating this semester. Then he explained that he had just been diagnosed with cancer. Now I was really concerned and shaken. We, of course, stopped talking about course-related concerns and discussed his prognosis, his fears, his challenges, and the like. My student did not yet know too many details. That evening, I called a friend who had won a battle with the same cancer and spoke with him at length, taking notes as to the options under various circumstances and so forth.

The next day on my way to class, I saw at a distance my cancer-stricken student, walking with his friends and happily joking. Soon he came to my office to discuss make-up work and so forth. I readily accommodated his requests. When I mentioned that I had talked at length with a friend who had a similar diagnosis, my student appeared sheepish, and said he had to hurry or be late for class. Not wanting to impose, I told him I was always available, and that I hoped to see him soon.

He got the make-up work done. Considering his stress, his performance in the class was admirable. He more than passed the course. I distributed his final grade sheet last, hoping that would give me a chance to inquire as to how he was doing. It was then, more sheepish than ever, that he informed me that he had been misdiagnosed, and was, in fact, fine after all.

I'll let you draw your own conclusions about what happened in this case.

But the more important question is this one: Would you as a teacher do anything differently if faced with a similar situation down the road?

I have affirmed that I would not. The benefits of being vulnerable as a teacher far outweigh the risks.

I need my students to know that I care about what we are working on together, and thus I care about them, even though I risk being taken advantage of. I want them to take risks when they approach learning new material, and to encourage them, I need to model such risk-taking myself, even as it leaves me open to criticism. No syllabus can ever make it totally safe for teachers, and maybe we should not be so invested in trying to make them so. Ultimately, for every one student who negatively takes advantage of our openness, there will be scores more who thrive because of it.

I have long argued that our students need not "like" us, except to the extent that their affection facilitates their trust in us. I also believe that students do not resent it when we challenge them with higher expectations, as long as they trust that we are fair and open. And, in order for them to trust me, I must trust them—as foolish as I may, or may not, appear when I am duped.

Because, far more often than not, vulnerability provides what's necessary for teachers and students to excel.

Reprinted with a new title from *The Teaching Professor,* Dec 2012

Something to think about…

"The classroom works best when students and teachers perceive it as a place where there is a continuing conversation among interested people…. A sense of community is not created by rules and laws, but by a sense of mutual respect and tolerance. Good neighborliness cannot be legislated—it can only be learned by example and experience, and it flourishes in an atmosphere of trust and acceptance of differences."

Reference: Singham, M. (2005). Moving away from the authoritarian classroom. *Change* (May/June), p. 57.

What to do when there's too much content to cover

More Content Doesn't Equal More Learning

by Nicki Monahan, George Brown College, Ontario

Reason to read: We desperately need new thinking about the role of content in courses and learning. Typically, it's the content that directs our instructional decision-making, and we need to challenge the assumption that more is always better when it comes to content. Here's an example of the kind of new thinking that retains the importance of content and proposes more viable ways to think about how much content is enough in courses.

With access to a world of information as close as our phones, it's easy to feel overwhelmed by all there is to teach. New material continues to emerge in every academic discipline, and teachers feel a tremendous responsibility not only to stay current themselves, but to ensure that their learners are up to date on the most recent findings. Add to this information explosion the passionate desire by faculty members to share their particular areas of expertise and it's easy to see why content continues to grow like the mythical Hydra of Greek legend. And like Hercules, who cut off one of Hydra's nine heads only to have two more grow in its place, faculty struggle to tame their content monsters.

The two most common strategies for managing course content rarely yield positive results. Cutting back or trimming content leads to agonizing decisions but does not produce substantive changes. Adding content to an already jam-packed syllabus puts us in a race to the course finish line—talking a mile a minute and leaving exhausted students in the dust. Learners in these scenarios liken the experience to trying to drink water from a fire hose. Hoarse, exhausted faculty and drowned, resentful students are not representative of the type of deep and meaningful learning that most of us aspire to.

Perhaps it's time to rethink the role of content in teaching and learning. A fresh perspective on this problem includes thinking about our role as faculty and that of our students, as well as reconsidering the nature of curriculum design.

The role of "content expert" is a familiar and comfortable one for most of us, and the many years spent gaining expertise in a discipline may make us reluctant to relinquish this position. Yet a narrowly defined role as content expert invariably leads to a "content coverage" model of teaching that puts information transmission at the heart of what we do. And while accessing knowledge is essential in learning, it is not the end of learning.

What our students need from us is assistance in navigating the waters of this ocean of information. We can become "content curators" who judiciously select the best "artifacts" for learning, much like the museum curator analyzes and documents all of the materials available before selecting the best representations for any given collection. Our students also need to learn the skills necessary to review and evaluate various sources of information—and to be able to differentiate what's relevant, accurate, and reliable, and why. If we teach research and critical thinking skills, our learners will develop the capacity to cope with information overload, a problem that is unlikely to disappear in the near future.

A realignment of our role from content expert to content curator also puts content itself into a new perspective. Rather than "covering" content, we use carefully selected content to help students develop the skills of their discipline or their profession. So, for example, students of history learn how to use primary sources to think like historians, and biology students learn to use a scientific approach for testing hypotheses.

With a shift in focus from *covering* content to *using* content, curriculum design also becomes less a matter of determining "what" to teach and more a matter of "how" to facilitate learning. Critical decisions about content still need to be made, but from a different perspective. One approach is to consider the scenario that Maryellen Weimer suggests: Imagine you meet a student five years after he or she took your course. What would you like to have that student remember from the course? Rather than being able to cite specific facts or information, I think we'd all much rather prefer that our former students remember key concepts that transformed their thinking. Often referred to as "threshold concepts," these ideas can become the cornerstones on which we organize our curriculum.

In addition to recognizing the importance of understanding threshold concepts, students might also look back and recognize that it was not knowledge itself that had the greatest impact, but the ability to apply that knowledge. They might remark on the capacity to utilize a formula to solve a problem or adopt a theoretical model to produce a finished product. If we begin with these demonstrated outcomes when designing our curriculum, then content becomes a vehicle by which we help students apply what they have learned.

This forward-thinking, backward-planning approach to curriculum development, which incorporates an understanding of threshold concepts, is a vital tool in the battle against content dominance. If we look to the future and carefully consider what we want our students to understand deeply by the time they successfully complete our course, then we can take a backward-design approach to create the learning experiences that will help them achieve that. If we continue to view content as that which needs to be covered rather than the fuel for meaningful learning, then we are destined to fight a losing battle.

Reference: Meyer, J.H.F., and Land, R. (2003). Threshold concepts and troublesome knowledge: Linkages to ways of thinking and practicing. In Rust, C. (ed.), *Improving Student Learning—Theory and Practice Ten Years On*. Oxford: Oxford Centre for Staff and Learning Development, 412–424.

Reprinted from Faculty Focus, Oct 12, 2015

Something to think about...

"Mostly, students do not get educated because they study our beloved content. They get educated because they learn how to study our beloved content, and they carry the how of that learning with them in the world as cognitive and intellectual skills that stick long after the content is forgotten." (p. 97)

Reference: Gregory, M. (2005). Turning water into wine: Giving remote texts full flavor for the audience of friends. *College Teaching*, 53(3), 95–98.

Why Don't We Teach the Telephone Book?

by Daniel J. Klionsky, University of Michigan

Reason to read: Sometimes the point that we're too committed to content coverage can be made with a bit of humor.

I don't get it! Telephone directories are filled with lots of information and with loads of new numbers, so why don't we design a class that covers this material? Why don't we expect folks to study these directories and memorize the numbers? For one thing, there are just too many numbers. Back when there were only a dozen or so, it might have been possible to memorize them all—not that it would have served any existential purpose, but just as an exercise. Now there are way too many. In fact, it turns out that most people have no interest in memorizing telephone numbers. They used to learn those numbers they regularly used, but cell phones have removed even that reason. Basically, all folks need to know is how to find a phone number.

It is unfortunate that the same logic is not applied to many of our science courses. I write about science because I know it firsthand, but I suspect this applies to many kinds of courses. First, our knowledge of biology (and many other fields) has increased tremendously over the past few decades, well beyond what any individual can hope to master, yet we continue to try to teach "all of it" in the standard biology curriculum. Sometimes there's no more justification other than that "we know it." A second problem is that people want information when they have a need for it. So, it is difficult or impossible to get students to want to learn course material if they do not see a practical use for it. Unfortunately, many college and university courses cover information that most students may never need to know, although many of my colleagues find that very difficult to admit.

Many upper-division courses contain information that is taught for no real purpose, at least not a purpose that is relevant for the students. These courses are taught for not very good reasons, such as because the department has a faculty member with a specialty in that area. I have sat in on many upper-division courses and wondered why the instructor was covering information that I did not know, and which I later discovered the instructor had only learned the day before while preparing the lecture. If practicing scientists do not know these details, why should undergraduate students be forced to learn them?

Louis Pasteur said, "Chance favors the prepared mind," and we do not know just what information will be important to us in the future. But I suggest that sentiment argues against courses that teach large amounts of factual information. Rather, we want our students to be prepared to deal effectively with whatever information—uncovered by chance or research—comes their way. Accordingly, we should not teach science (or other subjects) as though every fact is worth knowing, any more than we would use a telephone book to help us memorize numbers. Textbooks are full of useful information and are handy to have around when you need to look up a fact. Memorizing facts is not as important as knowing how to ask questions and how to synthesize information to formulate an answer. When we plan out our courses—and our entire curriculum—we should keep this in mind: How much of the information that we are going to cover do the students really need to know? How much time do we devote to making sure students know when they need a fact and how to look it up? Finally, and most importantly, do our students know what to do with the facts once they find them?

Reprinted from *The Teaching Professor*, Mar 2006

Something to think about...

"Once, the successful college student could be thought of in encyclopedic terms: all the facts, formulas, and theories neatly organized for quick and reliable retrieval. Today, though, a segment of the academy argues that the successful college student is much more a clever librarian—that is, someone who knows how to ask the right questions and to recognize good answers. This reformulation of knowledge, they say, is the practical recognition that no one has sufficient time or gray matter to master a knowledge base that is growing exponentially every decade or so."

Reference: Zemsky, R. *Inside Higher Education,* Sept 14, 2009

Assignments and grading policies shape learning experiences

Thinking about Writing Assignments Developmentally

Reason to read: The goals course assignments accomplish should change as students move through a curriculum. Too often, we have beginning students and seniors doing the same kinds of assignments. Here's an example of how writing assignment might evolve.

In the piece summarized here, the five authors describe the goals and offer illustrations of writing assignments developmentally appropriate for beginning, intermediate, and advanced psychology courses. Their justification makes sense in any discipline that relies on writing assignments. "If the psychology curriculum is developmentally structured to progress from introductory to advanced courses to foster student learning…, it is reasonable to argue that [students] may benefit from writing assignments that match this gradual increase in complexity." (p. 88) Most faculty do use assignments that reflect the level of the course, but not with the thoughtful planning and care illustrated by the assignments described in this article.

For **beginning courses,** the authors recommend "writing assignments that are brief in length (five pages or fewer, they note elsewhere), assigned frequently, and focused on assessing students' reflections and reactions to class reading and discussions…." (p. 89) In these papers, students offer opinions with at least some evidence to support them. They should start using the language of the discipline, but more important is the application of key concepts (psychological concepts, in this example) to daily life. Accepted disciplinary style guidelines (in this case, APA style) should not be required in these papers. The example discussed at length in the article is an analytical essay students write about an advertisement that involves race, class, gender, or sexuality. In the paper, they explore the psychological consequences of the images in the ad.

In **intermediate courses**, writing should "encourage significant personal engagement with the material, so that students synthesize ideas for a sub-discipline while also trying to express original ideas within its framework of reference." (p. 89) For psychology courses at this level, the authors recommend assignments that encourage reflection—but now, this should be reflection focused specifically on a question or issue related to the content area of the course. At this level, students should be expected to write using more disciplinary language and theory. They should also be writing with some understanding of methodology. These papers should be between five and ten pages long, correctly formatted in APA style. The example, from an Abnormal Psychology course, is 10-page paper on a disorder that interests the student and is taken from a list of possibilities provided in the syllabus. Students work on these papers in groups, but significant parts of the paper are prepared individually.

In **advanced courses,** writing assignments should focus on and continue developing the higher-order thinking skills of analysis and synthesis. Students should be able to offer critiques. Papers should move students in the direction of being able to produce knowledge, as opposed to simply consuming it. The recommended length for these papers is between 15 and 25 pages and students should (with teacher input) be able to generate their own topics. The most typical examples here are traditional research papers and honors theses.

Part of this article of interest to instructors teaching any subject is content that explores and illustrates the development of learning objectives for writing assignments. The authors note that "counter to what most students probably believe, it is not easy to design effective assignments. The development of meaningful and measurable learning objectives is challenging." (p. 95) Because of this, many instructors avoid doing so, or else they design the assignment first and generate learning outcomes after the fact or only when asked for them. Starting with the learning objectives—what it is students should know and be able to do—results in better-designed assignments and makes grading easier and more objective. The article contains examples of learning objectives that pertain to the intermediate assignment example and samples of grading rubrics used to assess the assignments.

They illustrate the value of being able to clearly connect assignments, goals, and grading criteria.

Reference: Soysa, C. K., Dunn, D. S., Dottolo, A. L., Burns-Gover, A. L., and Gurung, R. A. R. (2013). Orchestrating authorship: Teaching writing across the psychology curriculum. *Teaching of Psychology*, 40(2), 88–97.

Reprinted from *The Teaching Professor*, May 2013

Writing Good Assignment Descriptions

Reason to read: Are students regularly asking what you want in an assignment? If so, maybe your description of the assignment merits review.

Concern about the quality of student writing is ongoing and not without justification. Faculty are addressing the problem with more writing assignments and a concerted effort to improve student writing across the curriculum. Authors Allison Rank and Heather Pool, who during their graduate work directed a political science writing center, laud these efforts but point out that faculty are not looking carefully at the assignment descriptions they give students. "We argue that the intent, structure, and working of a prompt all help promote or impede student writing." (p. 675) In this very detailed article, they offer advice and suggestions on writing better assignment prompts. The article's many examples are drawn from political science, but the advice and suggestions offered are broadly applicable.

The authors aspire to give teachers guidance "about how to actually write a clear and doable writing assignment, pitched at the right level to achieve specific aims." (p. 676) They start with an updated version of the Bloom taxonomy, to which they add further modifications. Writing assignments can be designed to achieve five cognitive objectives, listed from low to high as in the Bloom hierarchy: 1) to summarize, which demonstrates a grasp of previously presented material; 2) to relate, which develops connections among concepts, events, and actors; 3) to analyze, which deconstructs arguments using logic and disciplinary standards; 4) to evaluate, which involves assessing claims according to disciplinary standards; and 5) to create, which involves generating content ranging from research questions to policy proposals. (p. 677)

They recommend appropriate terms for prompts at each of these levels and identify the benefits to students and instructors of each objective in a helpful table on page 677. Assignment terms should be used precisely. For example, the terms "describe" and "discuss" mean different things. Describe means "to give a detailed account," whereas "discuss" means to "offer a considered and balanced review that includes a range of arguments, factors, or hypotheses." (p. 676) To ask students to do both in a single question encourages preparation of confused and muddles responses.

The authors make the same point about an assignment that contains multiple questions. "Instructors often use a host of questions that seem to be clear and in order, but students frequently respond with paralysis." (p. 678) Beginning writers may struggle to identify the central and supporting questions, responding with papers that are not structured around a clear thesis statement. Authors Rank and Pool recommend identifying primary and secondary questions for beginning writers, and encouraging more advanced writers to consider the relationships between questions before they start writing. Differentiating between multiple questions as they write assignment prompts can also help instructors see if the goals of the assignment align with course objectives.

The article also contains a discussion of each of the five writing assignment cognitive objectives, which are summarized briefly here.

Summarize — "These prompts (define, summarize, describe, identify) require [students], in their own words, to communicate information covered in lectures, readings, or prior classes." (p. 678) The authors recommend using these prompts in low-stakes free writing assignments when the instructor needs feedback on the levels of student understanding. This writing can also be used in class to promote discussion.

Relate — "Asking students to *relate* two distinct analyses works best when they have been prepared by thinking about theories or events in conceptually related ways that are held together by major ideas or questions." (p. 678)

Analyze — Writing assignments of this sort involve disciplinary standards. Students are being asked to critically engage with course material by applying disciplinary rules for making and supporting arguments, for example. Students might be asked to "consider an argument or concept in a way that uncovers the assumptions and interrelationships of the issue." (p. 679) Writing assignments like these develop students' abilities to critically analyze.

Evaluate — Prompts that ask students to evaluate benefit them in three ways: 1) they are exposed to the standards of evidence-based inquiry; 2) they are asked to consider the implications of theories being discussed in the course; and 3) they do not have to simply accept conclusions offered by authorities, but are challenged to evaluate those conclusions.

Create — Here students do writing assignments in which they use the knowledge and skills they've gained through the course to create new knowledge. At the high end of the Bloom taxonomy, these are the most challenging writing assignments and the ones that require significant preparation before they can be successfully completed.

Beyond these five cognitive objectives for writing assignments, the authors make a strong case for writing assignments that ask students to reflect on their learning. "We encourage instructors who ask students to write multiple papers to also ask them to reflect on how the feedback on their first paper influenced their approach to the second." (p. 680)

The authors rightly observe that the literature is full of descriptions of different kinds of writing assignments, different ways those assignments can be integrated in non-writing courses, and different approaches to assessing writing, but there is precious little advice "about how we ask students to write." (p. 680) This very well-written article does an excellent job of filling that gap.

Reference: Rank, A., and Pool, H. (2014). Writing better writing assignments. *PS, Political Science and Politics,* 47(3), 675–681.

Reprinted from *The Teaching Professor,* Jan 2015

Grading Policies and the Principles of Solid Measurement

Reason to read: Here's the principles on which ethical grading policies should rest.

In an excellent article on "Helping Students Understand Grades," Marilla Svinicki recommends grading policies "based on solid measurement principles and common sense…" (p. 101)

Grading systems should be based on performance benchmarks. She's referring to the levels of performance represented by each of the major grading categories. This encompasses those aspects of a student's performance on an exam, in a paper, or on another assignment that qualify it as an A, B, C, or so on.

Grading systems should be valid and recognizable. Validity is the measurement term that refers to whether the measurement instrument (such as an exam, paper, group project, or any other assignment) is measuring what it's supposed to. Valid grading systems are tightly linked to course goals. Grades should be derived from achievement of those goals, but sometimes grading policies muddy those waters. Some would argue that teachers compromise the validity of their grading system when they incorporate things like attendance and participation into the grade.

Grading systems should be reliable. "The concept of reliability means that the measurement will give the same approximate results no matter how many times it's repeated or who does the scoring." (p. 102) It's really about objectivity, which is easiest to achieve when exams are multiple-choice, but more difficult when grading essays and short answers. Reliability is sometimes hard for students to understand. They will argue that another student said the same things in their answer, but that student got a higher grade.

The consistent application of a grading policy helps students accept that it's fair.

The grading system should be logical and based on real differences in performance. It should be a system that makes sense to students. The performance levels should be distinct. Students who get A's should be doing work at a different level than students getting B's and C's.

Reference: Svinicki, M. D. (1998). Helping students understand grades. *College Teaching,* 46(3), 101–105.

Reprinted from the supplementary materials accompanying the 20-Minute Mentor Program, "Grading Policy Essentials"

Recommended Resources

Schinske, J., and Tanner, K. (2014). Teaching more by grading less (or differently). *Cell Biology Education—Life Sciences Education,* 13 (Summer), 159–166.

These authors make a strong case against grading on a curve and offer an interesting history of grading.

Walvoord, B. E., and Anderson, V. J. *Effective Grading: A Tool for Learning and Assessment in College.* 2nd ed., San Francisco: Jossey-Bass, 2010.

Here's a classic work that covers a range of issues related to grading and grading policies. It's especially good when discussing how to establish criteria and standards for grading.

Taking your skills to the next level

Introduction

It's never been officially established how long you remain a "new" teacher or at what point you start the transition from newbie to expert. It's more a matter of where you feel you are. Wherever that might be, you've got skills that can be taken to the next level. All teachers can improve.

It also important to recognize that teaching skills aren't immutably fixed. They evolve and change, and that movement can be in two directions. Changes can mean more or less learning for students; they can make teaching more or less satisfying for you. This section focuses on positive skill development. It covers a range of topics that are important parts of your instructional health and well-being.

Teacher identity. Your style, sometimes called your teaching persona, is who you are when you teach. It's also who you want to be and how you become that person. Some new teachers (and those not-so-new) try to be like their best teachers and avoid those things done by their worst. This works, provided the teachers you're emulating have styles that fit comfortably with who you are. Others have in mind what they think students and/or colleagues expect teachers to be and work to confirm those expectations. This works too, so long as you're not pretending to be someone you aren't. Others just try to do what comes naturally, to be themselves.

There's a kernel of truth in the advice to just be yourself. The best teaching is always teaching that is a genuine, authentic representation of who you are, but with some important caveats. Teachers have professional responsibilities. They represent disciplines and showcase how professionals in that field act. For some teachers, this implies something about how they should dress. For others, it may be about how they speak. Beyond professional responsibilities, who you are as a teacher needs to expedite learning for students. If you're naturally pretty free-form without much need for structure and you're teaching a lot of beginning students who aren't academic superstars, your movement in and around points without much sense of direction can compromise their efforts to learn. Who you are must be shaped, in part, by who your students are. It's a complicated process and not one you only do once.

Improvement. Build on your strengths and learn from your mistakes. There's two ways you can improve your teaching. You can fix what isn't working, and you can do more of what is working. It's best not to base efforts to improve entirely on the premises of remediation and deficiency. If teacher improvement is only about fixing problems, that doesn't make it a very positive process or one regarding which you'd like to collaborate. Besides, if you focus on what is working, there's less time and space in your teaching for what isn't.

Improvement is not a dirty word. All teachers can improve. Improvement should be seen as an opportunity to learn, to grow and develop as a teacher. It's part of what makes teaching interesting, intellectually challenging, and intensely satisfying across the years. It lets you believe that that you haven't yet done your best teaching yet.

Teacher identity

Six Myths about a Teaching Persona

by Linda Shadiow and Maryellen Weimer

Reason to read: Finding your way to a teaching style that works is important both at the beginning of a teaching career and as it progresses. Doing so depends on understanding what a teaching persona is and why thoughtful consideration of yours matters.

What myths about constructing a teaching persona merit review? Teachers regularly exchange general advice about how to establish an identity in the classroom. Like most myths, these contain kernels of truth, but we believe their conclusions require a critical look. What are your beliefs about teaching persona, how it develops, and the role it plays in student learning?

Myth 1: Try to be like your own best teacher. "The best way to develop your persona is by doing what your best teachers did."

What if your best teacher isn't at all like you as a person? That teacher made an impact on you by drawing from his or her own character traits. In following this advice uncritically, you end up trying to be like someone else. Linda had a favorite teacher who used wry, sarcastic humor to comment on less-than-stellar assignments. When she tried to copy that in her own teaching, it came across as being accusatory rather than prodding. It's better to look at our favorite teachers and ask: "What did this teacher do that made me want to learn and helped me learn?" And then, "If that's my goal, how can I get there in a way that will work for me given the strengths I bring to teaching?"

Myth 2: Teach the course you'd like to take. "Teach the course using the approaches that motivated you and helped you learn successfully."

Are your classes full of students who are just like you when you were a student? We usually teach courses we did well in ourselves, courses with content that captured our imaginations and motivated us to work hard on mastering the material. When we choose approaches and strategies with the intent of reaching students like ourselves, we create a singular learning environment that will work for some students, but not for all. We can start with the features of courses we'd like to take, but the next question is, "What else is needed to promote the learning efforts of my students?"

Myth 3: Consider your teaching persona as a mask. "Teaching is really a performance and the classroom is a stage."

A mask may bear some resemblance to you, but in truth, masks are something you put on to hide who you are. We may be motivated to hide behind a mask because teaching makes us vulnerable and a mask offers protection. But masks hide a teacher's authenticity and students are good at detecting teaching that isn't genuine. Masks should motivate us to ask: "What am I hiding and why?"

Myth 4: Just do what comes naturally and your teaching persona will emerge. "You don't need to worry about it. Just be yourself."

A teaching identity will emerge out of doing what comes naturally, but will it be one that motivates and supports student learning? The classroom is not the family dinner table, where "doing what comes naturally" is appropriate. Sometimes our actions and behaviors can impede learning. They confuse students and be misunderstood. Take "what comes naturally" and ask how it can be adapted into attributes that contribute to an environment conducive to learning.

Myth 5: Start out being a tough teacher; establish that you are in charge. "If you don't get things set up properly in the beginning of the course, you can lose control, and once lost, it's very difficult to regain."

This myth speaks to the long-held stereotype of the stern, pointer-wielding, authoritative teacher who frightens students into a silent submission. Do you have evidence other than hearsay that a teacher who doesn't establish his or her credibility in forceful ways has classroom management issues? Does this myth speak to who you want to be as a teacher or who you think you need or ought to be? This myth is often accompanied by the advice that "you can always let up on them later." What are the consequences of dramatically shifting a persona midway through a semester?

What benefits would accrue if you started class by being who you want to be?

Myth 6: Teaching persona is not important enough to merit much attention. "Teaching is about student learning, their mastery of the material and development of intellectual skills. Compared to that, persona is a trivial and unimportant matter."

Students (especially beginning ones) identify more strongly with their teachers than teachers think they do. Teachers can easily stress students and compromise their confidence in learning. Ignoring your teaching persona can lead to unexpected consequences. For instance, even positive teacher attributes, like Maryellen's animated enthusiasm, can seem excessive and off-putting to students taking classes at her favorite teaching time, 8 a.m. The role teachers play in students' learning experiences is too important to ignore. We must continually examine who we are as teachers and what that contributes to the learning efforts of our students.

Reprinted from Faculty Focus, Oct 26, 2015

Something to think about...

Cranton and Carusetta write that when faculty look for teaching advice, they consult the how-to literature, be that a generic resource or something based in their discipline. "These resources serve faculty well, but they have one common flaw: They most often provide principles, guidelines, strategies, and best practices without taking into consideration individual teachers' personalities, preferences, values, and ways of being in the world—the ways in which they are authentic. The assumption underlying this approach is that what works well for one teacher in one context works well in general for all teachers in all contexts." (pp. 5–6)

The authors believe that teachers become authentic when they question what is right for them and develop their own unique style. This enables them to be genuine when they teach, and that authenticity allows them to connect with students in meaningful and motivational ways.

Reference: Cranton, P., and Carusetta, E. (2004). Perspectives on authenticity in teaching. *Adult Education Quarterly,* 55(1), 5–22.

Improvement as an opportunity for learning

Confessions of a Bad Teacher

Reason to read: It takes courage to admit in print that you aren't a good teacher. Here are some highlights from an article in which the author makes that admission. It's also the account of how he changes, builds a teaching identity that fits who he is, and makes it easier for students to learn.

It's not often an article starts with an admission like this: "I was a bad teacher." (p. 32) Can you see yourself submitting an article that begins this way? Definitely not before tenure and probably not even after that—is that what most of you are saying?

And what was it that made Mark Cohan a bad teacher? "I was not mean or abusive to students, and I didn't make capricious demands, ignore my syllabus, grade while under the influence, or test students on material I had not taught." (p. 32) But his course evaluations were not stellar, despite spending a great deal of time devoted to preparation. However, what signaled his ineffectiveness was how disconnected he felt from his students. "They were enigmas to me, and I didn't know how to deal with the varying levels of interest, commitment, and ability they brought to class. All I knew how to do was to expect of them what I had always expected of myself—not perfection, exactly, but something close to it." (p. 32)

Like many of us in academe, Cohan was raised in a middle-class family where school was a priority. It was expected that after high school, he would go to college. His parents paid for his education so he didn't need to work while in school. He gave school his full, undivided attention. "I had been taught my whole life to see myself in terms of grades and commitment to school and to judge myself harshly if either of those faltered; why wouldn't I see my students through the same lens?" (p. 34)

Cohan arrived at his first teaching job with high expectations for students, which they mostly failed to reach. He critiqued their performances, offering far more judgment than praise. He says that he lacked "the compassion, patience, and power necessary to help students meet those expectations." (p. 33)

But the problem really wasn't Cohan's students. "Truthfully, it was I who was not measuring up; I was not practicing the craft of teaching at a high level and, more importantly, I was not taking full measure of myself. I was not reflecting on who I was and how that could, would, or should inform who I was as a teacher." (p. 33) Once he started making that reflection an integral and ongoing part of his teaching practice, he was able to re-orient his teaching. "My own transformation has meant that I am much less a critic and much more a mentor to my students." (p. 33)

His transformation did not happen overnight, nor is it fully finished—nor has progress always been straightforward. He has arrived where he is now by stops and starts. Early on, a tutoring experience with one student gave him "a glimpse of a new conception of the teacher.

"What that experience produced was a shift in consciousness. The recognition (albeit intermittent and partial) that one fundamental flaw in my teaching—a source of the angst that infused my effort and daily wore me down—was inside me meant that I could actively work to change it." (pp. 34–35)

Cohan's insights about himself were affected by teaching experiences in a community college and at a small Jesuit university where teaching was taken very seriously. It was there his pedagogical knowledge began to grow. Attendance at workshops and conversations with teaching colleagues encouraged more thinking and reflection about his teaching—some of it decidedly painful. "Sometimes, all of this conferring and contemplation left me overwhelmed. I would become convinced that all of my course designs were broken beyond repair and that I would need a year…to scrap and rebuild them. In darker moments, I was convinced that I was broken beyond repair—a well-meaning but hopeless instructor who didn't have the gift."

But Cohan has made much progress. "I believe I've come quite a ways from my days of treating students like problem children and writing outlines on the board to avoid really interacting with them. The challenge for me…has been to stop projecting who I was as a student onto my students." (p. 36)

This is a truly amazing article, for any number of reasons. Many teachers begin where Cohan started, but few are willing to own up to the problems that beset those who teach from a place of superiority and impossibly high standards. Not only is this a journey from which others can learn, it's an optimistic piece. Teachers can change how they orient to teaching—not just around the edges with a few new techniques, but in a way that allows them to transform how they teach and what they believe about students.

Reference: Cohan, M. (2009). Bad apple: The social production and subsequent reeducation of a bad teacher. *Change* (November/December), 32–36.

Reprinted from *The Teaching Professor,* Feb 2010

On Becoming a Teacher

by Huntly Collins, La Salle University, Pennsylvania

Reason to read: Much can be learned from the thoughtful analysis of teaching experiences. Here's a new teacher whose first classroom experiences contain lessons that are reshaping her understandings of teaching and herself as a teacher.

The past three years have been a time of growth for me, some of it painful. I have become more humble and less arrogant. I have become less product-driven and more process-oriented. I have become less judgmental of my students' learning gaps and more engaged in helping them make up those gaps. I have learned not to teach to the middle just because most of my students are there, but rather to challenge everyone to go beyond where they think they can go. I have taken more risks and been less afraid to make mistakes. I have learned to worry less about students' perception of me and more about whether they are understanding what I am teaching. I have learned to let go of my preconceived ideas about students and to open myself to the surprises that each individual student has to offer.

I believe I have made a difference in the lives of my students; I know they have made a difference in mine. I have learned that teaching isn't about shiny new technology or well-organized lesson plans impressively arrayed in a binder. Although these help, teaching is really about being present for students and sharing with them the only thing we ultimately have to share, which is ourselves. Over the past three years, I have brought to my students all of the reporting and writing skills I accumulated over nearly a 30-year career as a reporter. I've shared my passion for the craft, its important role in giving a voice to the voiceless, and a sense of the great adventures that await those who learn to practice it well. I hope I have also given them a new appreciation for the power and beauty of the English language and imbued in them a desire to write well no matter whether they are going into journalism or some other profession or simply writing for their own pleasure.

Among the lessons learned as I've worked to grow as a teacher is that the process of learning is often as important as the end product. For me, this is a radical change. As a journalist, all that mattered to me and my editors was getting the story, getting it right, and telling it in a compelling way. All eyes were on the story, not on what I might have learned in the process of producing it. When I first arrived at La Salle, I put a similar emphasis on the end product in my journalism classes. Even though I tried to take into account the place from which students were starting, I focused almost exclusively on the quality of their stories, not on the process of their own development in getting the stories.

Today, however, I take as much pride in my students' sometimes halting efforts toward the goal as their ability to reach the goal. The terribly shy student who, despite his fears, stands to read his story to the entire class is engaged in important learning. The Dominican student who is writing in a second language may not turn out a perfectly polished story, but she becomes an effective communicator when she pulls at our heartstrings through the tale she tells. The C student, who seems oblivious to much of what I teach, emails me after she has graduated to ask, "What was that Robert Frost poem you read to us on our last day? I really want to remember one line." While that student may not have produced the best work in the class, she took away from the class something important, even if it was a single line from Frost's poem.

I've also learned that my students tend to under-value themselves, and one of the most important jobs I can do is to encourage them to be all they can be. A certain blue-collar mentality seems to pervade the student body— the idea that you're not supposed to be an intellectual or academically talented, so why even try? To address that, I've tried to expose students to the very best reporting and writing in America. I've also tried to give them more confidence in themselves, in the truth of their own experience, and in the power of expression. Some, miraculously, have responded. It has been truly wonderful to watch as students who never thought much about themselves have discovered, under my tutelage, that they have the potential to be excellent writers. "You mean, this is really good?" "Yes, it's really good. And here's how you can make it even better."

Teaching at La Salle has given me a few more gray hairs. But it has also made me wiser and more real.

Reprinted from *The Teaching Professor*, May 2009

Sustaining Excellence

Reason to read: Once acquired, teaching excellence must be sustained. Just because you've arrived there doesn't mean you get to stay.

"Sustained excellence seldom happens serendipitously. It is generally the result of a compelling vision, clear goals, careful planning, and a commitment to follow through. It often requires a willingness to embrace ambiguity, persist in the face of disappointments, adapt as necessary, and collaborate with diverse stakeholders."

The referent is teaching excellence—something we often think of as a destination, one of those places we aspire to reach. We tend to think that, like any destination, once you've arrived, you're there. The above quote highlights what's needed if you want to stay there; the work that brought you to that level of excellence must continue.

I also like the quote because it clearly spells out the actions required to sustain excellence. You don't remain an excellent teacher by wanting to be one in some amorphous, generic kind of way. Certainly, motivation is needed to drive your efforts, but the required efforts are specific. Excellence in the classroom is understood; that is, the teacher knows to what he or she aspires. Getting there is achieved via carefully set and clearly articulated goals. There's a plan in place for reaching those goals and the determination to do what needs to be done, step by step. This absolutely requires work, but the tasks involved are not impossible. They are not something attainable by only a few especially "gifted" teachers. More often than not, good teaching is achieved and sustained by teachers who are willing to make the effort.

Finally, the quote is powerful because it's honest about the efforts involved—not everything tried will be successful, not every decision is clear and unequivocal, not every choice will be a step forward. Our work as teachers is valued when we recognize how much rigor the task involves.

Reference: The quotation appears in a 2009 report, "Creating a Culture for Scholarly and Systematic Innovation in Engineering Education," published by the American Society for Engineering Education and may be found on the society's website.

Reprinted from *The Teaching Professor* blog, Jul 2009

"What Works" in the Messy Landscape of Teaching and Learning

Reason to read: Teaching would be a lot easier if we just knew "what works." We're looking for something we're not going to find.

The title is borrowed from text in an excellent article that challenges our use of the "what works" phrase in relation to teaching and learning. Biology professor Kimberly Tanner writes, "…trying to determine 'what works' is problematic in many ways and belies the fundamental complexities of the teaching and learning process that have been acknowledged by scholars for thousands of years, from Socrates to Piaget to more recent authors and researchers." (p. 329) Tanner proceeds to identify six reasons why the phrase hinders rather than fosters an evidence-based approach to teaching reform (in biology, her field, but these reasons relate to all disciplines). "Language is powerful," she notes. (p. 329) We use it to frame issues and when we do, it strongly influences our thinking about them.

"What works" is incongruent with the nature of science. Her point applies more broadly than to biology alone. The phrase implies that "what works" is readily applicable to all contexts. It also conveys the sense that once you know "what works," there is no need for further investigation. You've got the answer. There is no equivalent phrase or sentiment used in scientific investigations of the natural world, so "why should our evidence-based investigations and views about the issues in the teaching and learning of biology be any different?" (p. 330)

"What works" ignores individual students and their brains as key variables. If the solution works, then it works for all students, or at least most of them. Many studies document that "what works" for students depends on a host of demographic variables, including gender, language background, levels of family education, and ethnic identity. We must also consider the individuality of student brains, which Tanner describes as "individual both in terms of architecture and information previously stored within." (p. 330) "What if the right way to teach is not any singular way, but rather the use of a variety of teaching techniques intertwined to benefit a range of learners and their experiences in a heterogeneous classroom? What if the closest we get to 'what works' is to teach using all of the available techniques and not just one?" (p. 330)

"What works" assumes uniformity in instructor experience and skill. Also lurking within the "what works" assumption is the premise that it "works" for all instructors. Interestingly, when a technique is tried and it doesn't work, blame is usually affixed to the technique, not the instructor. For example, this might be taken to imply that "group work" is a bad technique, not that it was used ineffectively in a particular class. The success of instructional strategies, especially complex ones, depends on the experience and skill of the instructor. Any given technique may work, but not all instructors may be able to make it work, given their teaching skill and experience.

"What works" requires defining what is meant by "works." This problem with the phrase has two parts, accounting for two of Tanner's six reasons. The first is that the definition for "what works" is largely left to the user. Typically, "what works" means that the strategy or technique promotes learning as measured by test scores and course grades. Tanner points out that grades may improve using a given technique, but at the same time, the technique may have had no effect on student motivation or interest in the discipline.

The second definitional problem with the "what works" phrase and accompanying thinking is that evidence supporting the effectiveness of a particular solution is often based on short-term measures, typically grades. "'What works' for short-term performance in a course…may or may not be the same as 'what works' for deep conceptual change and long-term retention, yet we have little to no evidence beyond a single-semester timeframe." (p. 332)

Building a common language about the substance of the "what" in "what works" is not trivial. There is no common lexicon for instructional strategies. We toss strategy names about, assuming we all define them similarly, but in execution, even simple strategies like think-pair-share look very different. If that's true for comparatively straightforward techniques, imagine the variation involved in complex strategies like problem-based learning or in whole approaches like learner-centered teaching.

In sum, Tanner explains that "at some level, 'what works' arises from a desire to give scientists [and the rest of us] a shortcut to effective teaching, but there may not be any shortcuts." So what should we be saying and thinking in lieu of this phrase? "We can perhaps refocus on what has been shown again and again to be the path to effective teaching and learning: the development of reflective instructors who are analytical about their practice and who make iterative instructional decisions based on evidence from students sitting right in front of them." (p. 329)

Reference: Tanner, K. D. (2011). Reconsidering "what works". *Cell Biology Education,* 10 (Winter), 329–333.

Reprinted from *The Teaching Professor,* Feb 2012

Why Are We So Slow to Change the Way We Teach?

Reason to read: Some aspects of instruction are easy to change. The really substantive parts of what teachers do, however, are not so simple to change and how we think about change can make it even harder.

Some thoughts about change—not so much what to change as the process of change, offered in light of its slow occurrence.

Yes, lecture is a good example. In a recent survey, 275 economics faculty who teach principles courses reported they lectured 70 percent of the class time, led discussion 20 percent of the time, and had students doing activities for 10 percent of the time. The article cites studies in that field from the mid-'90s reporting similar percentages. Maybe some other specialties have changed more, but evidence supports a continuing reliance on lecture in many fields.

However, lecture isn't the only example of where we're slow to change. Many aspects of teaching—course design, approaches to testing, assignments, and grading—have also changed little. Granted, some faculty do change, a lot and regularly, but not the majority. The question is, "Why?" Here are some possibilities I've been considering.

Change is harder than we think. We are incredibly vested in our teaching, and, like our students, we are error-averse. Try something new, and there's a risk of failure. There's risk with what we do every day, but it feels safer to go with the tried and true. And most of the time, what's new has to be revised, tweaked, and further refined. First time through, it doesn't go as smoothly as what we're used to doing.

The work being done in cognitive psychology on the use of deliberate practice to develop expertise is relevant here. This is practice with specific characteristics: it involves difficult tasks that require focus and effort to achieve. Developing expertise also involves work on specific components of a task. There is a need for feedback from a coach with the ability to analyze the performance and propose how it can be improved. Meanwhile, the learner must reflect on both the performance and the feedback. As the name implies, deliberate practice means planned, purposeful practice, a consistent and concerted effort to improve.

Faculty tend to underestimate the complexity involved in changing their teaching. They approach it with a Nike-style "just do it" attitude. That can-do attitude is spot-on, but the approach to change is too often piecemeal and reactive. "Oh, that sounds like a good idea. I'll try that." Or "Gee, that might be a potential fix," for whatever problem is occurring. The hodge-podge infusion of new techniques, interesting ideas, and promising strategies circles around effective teaching rather than moving toward it with a map and designated route.

The "just do it" approach implies implementation before a consideration of goals—what the change will accomplish and how to figure out whether it does. A range of issues bear on the challenges of assessing change. Many of us have unrealistic expectations for success. We want the change to work perfectly right from the start—a "top 10" learning experience for every student and in every course. We are noble in our aspirations but unrealistic about outcomes. We then find that instructional changes don't work perfectly. But then, how often do we assess the results beyond our view of how it went down? In private, we question our ability; in public, we pin problems on the approach and/or the students.

We make change harder by going it alone. Do we discuss details with anyone beforehand? Do we contemplate the possibility of calling on a coach or mentor? Do we solicit feedback from students? More often, I'm sure, we implement and assess changes in isolation.

Uncomfortable with the implementation and disappointed in the results, we give up on the change, which rounds back to how vulnerable failure makes us feel. Wieman and Gilbert describe a large grant-funded project that involved the implementation of changes in 160 courses. They report that "roughly 100 hours" of practice were needed to switch to using new teaching methods effectively. I'm not sure how that figure was derived, but it makes clear that trying something on the fly once or twice is not likely to have the enduring effects we envision.

How we make changes isn't the only reason so much of what's done in the classroom stays the same, but it's a reason we can do something about.

References:
Goffe, W. L., and Kauper, D., (2014). A survey of principles instructors: Why lecture prevails. *Journal of Economic Education,* 45(4), 360–375.

Wieman, C. and Gilbert, S., (2015). Taking a scientific approach to science education, part II—changing teaching. *Microbe Magazine,* 10(5), 203–207.

Reprinted from The Teaching Professor blog, Feb 3 2016

Something to think about...
As Peter Filene writes in a chapter called, "Understanding Yourself as a Teacher:" "No teacher closes this chapter once and for all. Personal identity is a process, not a formula. As one inhabits new stages of life and new roles, one's sense of self evolves. However you define yourself as a teacher now, you will redefine it in the course of years and courses to come." (p. 12)

Reference: Filene, P. *The Joy of Teaching: A Practical Guide for New College Instructors.* Chapel Hill, NC: The University of North Carolina Press, 2005.

CHAPTER 2

Course Design Principles

When you've got a course to design or one to plan

Introduction

It's your course, which means you decide on the content, the assignments, testing mechanisms, you set up the terms and conditions for learning, and you decide how you're going to teach it. It's best not to start with by reinventing the wheel. Check out what others who have taught the course have done—in your department, at your institution, and elsewhere. Check out what's available online. Many disciplinary association websites have collections of syllabi and other course planning materials. Make it your own course, but don't be afraid to borrow and build on what others have done. Most course designs are not copyrighted.

Design details do make a difference. Currently it's popular to use a backward design approach. You start with what you want students to know and be able to do at the end of the course. You work backwards from there through assignments and activities to the content you'll use to accomplish your goals. Too often, teachers start (and end) with the content, which makes it the end, not the means through which learning occurs and skills are developed.

For those teaching part-time, you often don't get to design the course you're teaching. The content may be already designated, the text chosen, and the assignments set out. If it's not already clear, start by finding out how much, if any, discretion you do have. Can you fuss with the assignments? Can you change the content order? Can you substitute other readings? Even if you can't change much, you still need to make the course your own. Be your own person. Use those instructional strategies and approaches that you can execute well and that you know from previous experiences help students learn. If you're brand-new to teaching (and even if you're not), check Chapter 8 for ways to solicit feedback from students about their learning experiences.

Backward Design, Forward Progress

by Pete Burkholder, Fairleigh Dickinson University, NJ

> *Reason to read: A lot of instructors design the course while they write the syllabus. As important as the syllabus is to a well-run course, it's not the best template for course design. It's smarter to start with where you want to end and work from there back through the design details.*

Backward design, most often connected with such researchers as Grant Wiggins, Jay McTighe, and Dee Fink, asks faculty to initially ignore the specific content of a class. Rather, the designer begins the process by identifying desired learning goals, then devising optimal instruments to measure and assess them. Only after that does course-specific content come into play—and even then, it is brought in not for the sake of "covering" it, but as a means to achieve the previously identified learning objectives. Courses designed like this put learning first, often transcend the traditional skillset boundaries of their discipline, and usually aim to achieve more ambitious cognitive development than do classes that begin—and often end—with content mastery as their primary focus. Although the advantages of backward design are manifest, it's probably still the exception to, rather than the rule of, course planning.

Yet backward design has benefits beyond those outlined above. Just as the technique is advantageous to the students we teach, it is valuable to our own growth trajectory as educators, and serves as a useful bridge to interactions with faculty outside of our disciplines.

Making tough decisions

First, (re)designing a course via backward design forces us to step back from our fields of expertise, which we know so well and hold so dear, and approach the learning process as novices. That is to say, we are so familiar with our disciplines and their content that it's hard to imagine anyone not endowed with such knowledge or a burning desire to acquire it. Even more importantly, we love the content that makes up our fields, and it can be downright painful to imagine excluding parts of it for the sake of skill development or the realities of semester time limits.

Backward design forces us to make tough decisions about what content is really necessary for our students to achieve their learning goals. Maryellen Weimer writes that our attitude toward basic content "has always been dominated by one assumption: more is better" (p. 46). If that construct embodies the typical "coverage" approach, then perhaps "just enough content—and no more" could define the course built around backward design principles. When forced to make fundamental decisions about learning and the role of basic content therein, we must confront the very nature of what we seek to achieve as educators. Is it simply for students to know a lot about our field? Or is it primarily for them to develop the habits of mind that typify practitioners? The former aims low at the Bloom's Taxonomy target, while the latter requires an elevated trajectory.

Ken Bain writes about "expectation failure" (p. 28) as a necessary component to students' cognitive breakthroughs. That is, students must be placed in a situation where they realize their extant ways of knowing won't serve them adequately. Only then can they make their way through the "learning bottlenecks" (in the language of Díaz et al.) which populate our fields. I'd like to push Bain's analogy further: it is often only through our own expectation failures that we as faculty can devise more authentic and meaningful learning experiences for our students. For better or for worse (and usually it's for worse), most of us started out teaching the way we'd been taught ourselves—and many of us still do. Only when we realize that these approaches can't achieve our desired learning goals do we stare into the instructional abyss to contemplate the fundamental riddles of education. If we're lucky, we can seek help from a peer, or stumble across a good pedagogical read. And if backward course design is deemed a solution, we just might squeeze through our own instructional bottleneck and offer something so much better.

Breaking down silos

Second, it is precisely this type of work—the fumbling, the grappling, the eureka moment—that allows us to bridge the chasms between ourselves and faculty in other fields. Too often we remain siloed in our disciplines, knowing little about what our brethren do and assured they couldn't possibly understand us. But if we momentarily remove discussion of specific course content and focus instead on desired learning goals, we find that we actually have a great deal in common. Is clear and correct writing a goal only of composition classes? *(Of course not.)* Do we relegate critical thinking to the field of logic? *(I sincerely doubt it.)* Are group work, information literacy, and quantitative reasoning skills that can be developed and synergized across a broad spectrum of classes in disparate fields? *(Absolutely.)* Conversations and workshops about backward design necessarily raise these issues, help us emphasize the commonalities (rather than the differences) of seemingly unrelated fields, and serve as vehicles for interdisciplinary empathy and cooperation in ways that content-based curriculum development fails to do.

In the 1998 film *Patch Adams*, Robin Williams plays a physician with quirky but effective approaches to helping his patients. When questioned about his focus on the patient rather than the disease, he replies, "You treat a disease, you win, you lose. You treat a person, I guarantee you you'll win, no matter what the outcome." There's a parallel here for course design. Lead with content and maybe the more ambitious learning happens, maybe it doesn't. Lead with learning goals, as epitomized by backward design, and educational outcomes can't help but have an impact on students' development. And through adopting such a scheme, we become a more self-aware and interconnected faculty. It's hard to see a downside.

References:

Bain, K. (2004). *What the Best College Teachers Do*. Cambridge: Harvard University Press.

Díaz, A., Middendorf, J., Pace, D., and Shopkow, L. (2008). The History Learning Project: A department "decodes" its students. *Journal of American History*, 94(4), 1211–1224

Fink, L. D. (2003). *Creating Significant Learning Experiences*. San Francisco: Jossey-Bass.

Patch Adams (1998). Dir. Tom Shadyac. Universal Pictures.

Reprinted from Faculty Focus, May 16, 2016

Recommended Resource

Whetten, D. A., (2007). Principles of effective course design: What I wish I had known about learner-centered teaching 30 years ago. *Journal of Management Education*, 31(3), 339–357.

A great resource if you'd like to learn from someone who, like many of us, didn't take course design all that seriously when he first started teaching. If you aspire to use active learning and other learner-centered approaches, Whetten offers sound advice on making them part of the course design

Something to think about...

Too often, the selected textbook defines the course scope, sequence, and depth. Many instructors implicitly adhere to the view that a textbook's inclusion of information, in part, legitimizes teaching that content. Textbooks exert a significant influence on how content is taught—from the sequence of material to the manner in which it is presented. The issue here is not the value of textbooks, but rather the role they play in determining the curriculum and mode of instruction. Textbooks should be a tool to assist in learning, but they should not dictate the scope, sequence, and pedagogy in a course.

Reference: Clough, M. P., and Kauffman, K. J. (1999). Improving engineering education: A research-based framework for teaching. *Journal of Engineering Education* (October), 527–534.

PowerPoint: Key Considerations

Reason to read: Planning a course involves preparing a variety of materials, which also need to be carefully designed. If, in your case, that means PowerPoint slides, designing effective ones begins with understanding what they do and don't accomplish.

If you use PowerPoint in your classroom, you are certainly not alone. Sixty-seven percent of a 384-student cross-disciplinary cohort reported that all or most of their instructors use PowerPoint, and another 23 percent said that at least half of their instructors used it. A survey of faculty (a much smaller cohort) confirmed what students reported: 91 percent of the faculty said they use PowerPoint at least some of the time; 55 percent reported using it in at least three-quarters of their classes.

These faculty said they used PowerPoint to share lecture notes with students, show charts, offer definitions, and for explanation. A bit more than half embed video clips in their PowerPoint presentations. Students agreed: more than 80 percent said that "slideware is most useful when it is used to outline lecture notes and information." (p. 246) And 82 percent said they always, almost always, or usually copy information from the slides.

When asked what they disliked about PowerPoint, 32 percent of the students surveyed said they didn't like it when the professor read the material on the slides word for word. 24 percent disliked how using PowerPoint allows instructors to lecture faster, changing slides before they have the chance to get all the material copied down. In comments, they regularly noted how they struggle to copy the material and listen to the professor at the same time.

Despite these two objections, which were the most frequently mentioned negative features of PowerPoint, these students were overwhelmingly positive about the presence of PowerPoint. "Eight-four percent of these students agreed that the technology improves their overall classroom experience; only 9 percent said it did nothing to enhance their learning. Almost 70 percent preferred classes where teachers used PowerPoint compared with 10 percent who preferred classes without technology." (p. 248)

Even though these survey results indicate widespread use of and appreciation for PowerPoint, the authors raise several concerns which explains their ambivalent feelings about it. In their review of the research, they did not find studies documenting that PowerPoint has a positive, measurable influence on course performance. In most studies, its effect on grades is minimal. How can it be that something this highly valued for the way it organizes and clarifies content is not influencing measures of learning?

The authors discuss a "tension" that exists between PowerPoint as a vehicle that clarifies information and as a vehicle that oversimplifies it. One faculty comment makes the point clearly. "PowerPoint simplifies and dumbs down the info for them into neat little bullet points. The reality of our social world is often messier and more complicated than that which can be expressed by neat little bullet points." (p. 251)

Faculty also worry that PowerPoint decreases classroom interaction; it may do so for a few reasons. First, when students are focused on copying down what's on the PowerPoint slide, they are not thinking about the material. "Classrooms in which students take notes instead of actively engaging with material are little different from movie theaters—both are arenas of passive entertainment rather than active knowledge construction." (p. 251) If students are focused on getting what's on the slides down in their notes, they are not thinking about questions they might need or want to ask.

Classroom interaction is also diminished because PowerPoint shapes instruction. The slides are arranged in a particular order. Another faculty comment explains how that influences what teachers do. "Occasionally, I discuss topics in a different order than I originally planned, one that makes more sense in the context of a class discussion or a student question. That can be difficult to coordinate with PowerPoint. Sometimes I feel like I have to 'teach to the PowerPoint.'" (p. 252) In other words, students' questions can disrupt how the teacher has structured the material. Teachers may be reluctant to address a student comment that takes the discussion in a different direction. As a consequence, there can be less spontaneity in PowerPoint teaching.

These findings and concerns do not mean that PowerPoint is bad and to be avoided. Rather, PowerPoint is like any other instructional tool. How it affects learning depends on how teachers are using it. And that's the real merit of research like this: it challenges teachers and students—and, for that matter, to think about how PowerPoint is being used and whether it's promoting the kind of deep, lasting learning that is the goal of every course and teacher.

Reference: Hill, A., Arford, T., Lubitow, A., and Smollin, L. M. (2012). "I'm ambivalent about it": The dilemmas of PowerPoint. *Teaching Sociology,* 40(3), 242–256.

A revised version reprinted from *The Teaching Professor,* Oct 2012

Keeping courses fresh and effective

Introduction

It's a course you've taught a lot—maybe you teach it every semester, sometimes multiple sections a semester. Courses get tired and instructors can get tired of them. In general, this is not a sign that you need to exit the profession. One solution is to redesign the whole course. Toss out what you've been doing and start over. But that's a time-consuming endeavor and it may not be necessary. Often, there are small changes you can make that will refresh the course, making it feel new to you and students. The suggestions offered in this section are some of many possibilities. It's good to remember that courses don't stay the same even if you're teaching them the same way.

A Course Redesign Improves Attitudes and Performance

Reason to read: Here's evidence that course redesign activities can change learning outcomes in a course. It's also an example of how much needs to change once a course gets in trouble.

It is often difficult for teachers to face up to the fact that a course is in trouble—that students are complaining, unmotivated, and not learning the material at the level they should. This admission is even more difficult when it's a course for majors. But once the facts are faced, most of what makes courses ineffective can be fixed, or at least significantly improved.

Such was the case with the second semester of a two-sequence biology course required for majors and premedical students. The problems were not all that unusual for a large course enrolling between 170 and 190 students: lectures described by students as boring, failure to see the relevance of course content, more interest in grades than learning, poor attendance, and limited participation.

The course redesign involved changes in three areas. First, some of the course content was reordered. Next, active learning and group problem-solving were incorporated into the course. Students were formed into four-person groups that sat together throughout the semester. Almost every class session, students worked on a problem in these groups. Some group members were randomly selected to give a report after each group activity. Clickers were used, and some of the questions students were asked were samples from the Graduate Record Exam (GRE) and Medical College Admissions Tests (MCAT); the questions were labeled as such, which motivated students to attempt answers. Students earned participation points (20 out of a course total of 700) if they answered at least 75 percent of the clicker questions—regardless of whether their answers were correct. And finally, some student-centered pedagogy was used in the course. Learning goals were listed explicitly in lecture PowerPoint slides. Students got sets of vocabulary terms for each lecture to help them identify and focus on important concepts. A system of weekly quizzes was added to provide "low-stakes" feedback and encourage students to keep up with the material.

And what kind of results did these changes produce? First, student attitudes improved. Scores indicated they were more interested in the course material and better saw its relevance; students themselves reported that they were learning more and thought the classroom presentations were more stimulating, among other positive changes. These results emerged from survey data and on student course evaluations. An analysis of their open-ended responses collected before and after the course was redesigned revealed that the proportion of positive comments increased from 65 percent for the old course to 81 percent and 89 percent for the two years of the revised course.

In addition to better attitudes, there was also a positive change in student performance as measured by scores on identical final exam questions. Moreover, responses to open-ended questions on the final were rated using the Bloom taxonomy. In the unrevised version of the course, 82–85 percent were at levels 1 and 2 on the Bloom taxonomy. That percentage dropped to 75 for answers at the end of the revised course. Researchers concluded, "Our data on academic performance are consistent with previous studies indicating that student-centered pedagogy and interactive-learning activities increase student performance." (p. 211)

The research team, which included the professor who taught the course, acknowledge that the changes required a significant time commitment the first time they were implemented, but they describe this as a "one-time investment." (p. 212) Elsewhere, they write, "Our positive results illustrate how changing the instructional design of a course, without wholesale changes to course content, can lead to improved students attitudes and performance."

Finally, there was one more "unanticipated" benefit to this redesign effort. "It improved not only the students' attitudes toward the course, but also the instructor's morale and enthusiasm. Introductory Biology II has long been a problematic course for department because of the deficiencies noted in the introduction. As a consequence, instructors often lose enthusiasm for teaching this course after two to three years. However, the interactive pedagogy and positive student responses made this a much more exciting and rewarding course to teach in 2007 and 2008." (p. 212)

Reference: Armbruster, P., Patel, M., Johnson, E., and Weiss, M. (2009). Active learning and student-centered pedagogy improve student attitudes and performance in introductory biology. *Cell Biology Education,* 8 (Fall), 203–213.

Revised version reprinted from *The Teaching Professor,* Nov 2010

Refresh Your Course without (Too Much) Pain and Suffering

By Rebecca Brent, Educational Designs, Inc.

Reason to read: Need something to guide your efforts to refresh a course you regularly teach?

See if this sounds familiar. You're scheduled to teach a course you have taught before that desperately needs revision. The content and pedagogy go back for a decade or more and are both sadly obsolete, or the grades have been abysmal and the students are threatening to revolt, or someone (the department head, a faculty committee, or you) has decided to offer the course online, or maybe you're just bored and dread the thought of teaching it again.

We've all been there. It's time to revise the course, but with little extra time to spare, the task seems daunting. It doesn't have to be! A few relatively straightforward design changes can give any course new life, and you don't have to do it all at once. Often, the best approach is to spread the changes out over several semesters.

Step 1: Identify your reasons for change. Take a little time to think about the last time you taught the course and what problems you noted. Maybe student performance was not at the level you wanted, or elements of the course seemed out of date or boring. You can review student feedback on the course and see whether they had suggestions you'd like to try or concerns you want to address.

Step 2: Gather ideas and resources. Here you have lots of choices. Check with colleagues. Pay a visit to your Center for Teaching and Learning. Scan journals and conference proceedings. Look for online materials, such as course syllabi and handouts, as well as course-relevant videos, screencasts, simulations, case studies, and interactive tutorials. You can find a whole host of quality materials by searching digital resource libraries (e.g., YouTube, Wikimedia Commons, Khan Academy, MERLOT, the National Science Digital Library, and the National Center for Case Study Teaching in Science), and by entering "[type of resource][topic]" into a search engine like Google or Bing. Photos can spark new interest in a topic and the Creative Commons on Flickr has a rich collection of images.

If you're contemplating changes in a class you're currently teaching, enlist students in finding relevant resources for a few points on the next exam or homework assignment. (Many of our students are better at navigating the Internet than we are, and they'll do a lot for a couple of points.) Sometimes something as simple as a new resource can help to perk up a tired course.

Step 3: Plan the changes. Some changes require little planning at all—you just make them. Others, like flipping a class or incorporating a problem-based learning approach, may take several semesters to plan and implement. Here are a few relatively simple but effective things you might do:

- Add connections between course content and students' interests and prior knowledge.
- Incorporate technology resources you found in Step 2 into the course instruction.
- Mix it up. If your course involves selecting materials as bases for instruction and discussion (such as readings in a language or literature course), introduce a few new selections.
- Use active learning to enhance students' knowledge acquisition and skill development and to reduce their boredom and yours (Felder & Brent, 2009).
- Begin or increase instruction in critical and/or creative thinking (Fogler, LeBlanc & Rizzo, 2014; van Gelder, 2005).

You might also want to begin transitioning to a new, more powerful, but more complex teaching practice than you have been using. Such strategies as flipping your classroom (Brame, n.d.) going through case studies (NCCSTS), giving team assignments and projects (Major, 2015), or using problem-based learning (Prince & Felder, 2007) can be transformative, albeit challenging. To get started, develop a step-by-step plan over several semesters and make use of support resources like teaching center consultants, books, journals, online how-to webinars, and workshops to hone your expertise.

Step 4: Plan the evaluation. When you change a course, the one thing you can be sure of is that you won't get it right the first time. It's important to have an evaluation plan to determine the effects of the changes so you'll know which changes to keep, which ones to modify, and which ones to drop the next time you teach the course. Two evaluation strategies are especially helpful:

1. Immediately after a class session, spend a few minutes in your office going through the session plan and reflecting on lecture segments, questions, and activities. Make note of what worked and didn't and what changes you will make next time you teach the course.
2. Conduct a midterm evaluation that specifically asks students whether they think the new or modified features of the course helped their learning, hindered their learning, or did neither.

Step 5: Carry out the plans. Now you're ready to make the changes you planned, evaluate their effectiveness, and enjoy the fruits of your efforts. If you reflect on your classes, stay open to new teaching ideas, and try them out thoughtfully, you'll find your teaching continues to improve over time and teaching that familiar course will be something you look forward to.

References:

Brame, C.J. (n.d.). Flipping the classroom. Center for Teaching at Vanderbilt University. Retrieved from https://cft.vanderbilt.edu/guides-sub-pages/flipping-the-classroom/

Felder, R. M. & Brent, R. (2009). Active learning: An introduction. *ASQ Higher Education Brief,* 2(4), August. Retrieved from www.ncsu.edu/unity/lockers/users/f/felder/public/Papers/ALpaper(ASQ).pdf

Fogler, H. S, LeBlanc, S.E., & Rizzo, B. (2014). *Strategies for creative problem solving* (3rd ed.). Upper Saddle River, NJ: Pearson.

Major, C. H. (2015). Choosing the best approach for small group work. *Faculty Focus.* Retrieved from www.facultyfocus.com/articles/effective-teaching-strategies/choosing-the-best-approach-for-small-group-work/

National Center for Case Study Teaching in Science (NCCSTS). (n.d.). National Center for Case Study Teaching in Science. Retrieved from http://sciencecases.lib.buffalo.edu/cs/

Prince, M. J., & Felder, R. M. (2007). The many faces of inductive teaching and learning. *Journal of College Science Teaching,* 36(5), 14–20. Retrieved from www4.ncsu.edu/unity/lockers/users/f/felder/public/Papers/Inductive (JCST).pdf van Gelder, T. (2005). Teaching critical thinking: Some lessons from cognitive science. *College Teaching,* 53(1), 41–46.

Recommended Resource

Van Auken, P., (2011). Maybe it's both of us: Engagement and learning. *Teaching Sociology,* 41(2), 207–215.

The author had a major assignment in the course that wasn't producing student engagement and learning at the levels he'd hoped for. The article describes the thoughtful, systematic way he redesigned that assignment and what the new version of the assignment accomplished.

Handouts that Encourage Active Participation

Reason to read: Any aspect of a course can be redesigned. Here's an interesting redesign of the handouts used in a course.

Encouraging active participation is a tall order for handouts, especially given the downloadable, fully detailed handouts that most students seem to prefer. But that's what faculty member Keith Jakee claims can happen with the approach he takes to developing handouts for the technical content of his courses.

The handouts accompany his lectures, but he notes that he uses them "in a profoundly altered state from the ones commonly used. I take care to omit all of the most critical details that will be completed throughout the lectures itself." (p. 99) Rather, his outlines provide only the main contours

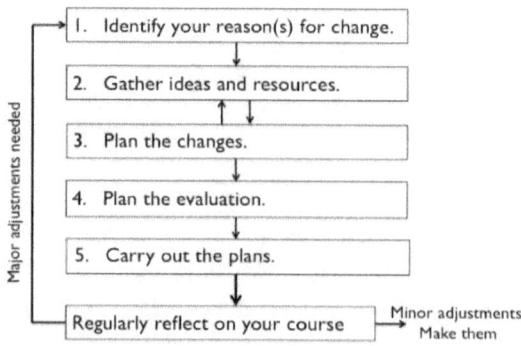

of the lectures. They give students a roadmap to follow as he moves them through the content. He does include material on the handouts that enables the efficient use of time during the lecture. Teachers should not waste time "dictating data" to students, so his handouts do include data, tables, and graphs. But sometimes only part of this material is provided so that students must fill in missing data as he presents it during the lecture. The article includes several samples of these handouts, showing what information the students receive initially and what information the instructor adds during the lecture.

Jakee discusses a number of benefits that accrue when handouts are designed with less, rather than more, information. These handouts do a better job of maintaining students' attention. They don't have to struggle with organization—they know where they've been and where they are going next. This enables them to focus on the material being presented. Moreover, a collection of these handouts ends up being a kind of workbook for the course, expediting the study and review process.

Second, designing handouts using these principles helps with class attendance. According to the author, "A very important feature of these handouts is they are useless without coming to class. Because upwards of 80 or 90 percent of the material is presented in the classroom, obtaining the handouts cannot serve as a substitute for the lecture itself." (p. 106) If very detailed lecture handouts are used, it is easy for students to think that everything they will need to know is on the handout and, therefore, missing class will not matter.

Jakee also maintains that the handouts increase student participation in the classroom. Because such handouts encourage students to keep up with the instructor, they are focused on and thinking about the material at hand. "The process is carefully choreographed so students can feel as though they are a step ahead of the instructor instead of waiting passively for the next piece of information to be handed to them." (p. 106)

The final benefit is one that both the instructor and students enjoy: these handouts require careful organization of lecture content. Jakee admits that they are initially time-consuming to prepare. But as a result, he comes to class with carefully organized material that enhances delivery of the content. For students, course content is more easily mastered because it is clear. It is also linked to what they've learned in previous class sessions.

The research on note-taking recommends using skeleton notes that give students some, but not all, of the material. Students need to interact with the content rather passively receiving it. What do students do with complete sets of notes provided by the instructor? They tend to memorize them and, as we all know, material can be memorized without being understood.

Reference: Jakee, K. (2011). Overhauling technical handouts for active student participation: A model for improving lecture efficiency and increasing attendance. *International Journal of Teaching and Learning in Higher Education*, 23(1), 98–108.

A revised version reprinted from *The Teaching Professor*, Nov 2011

CHAPTER 3

•

Students and Learning

Introduction

When students are missing basic skills and their behaviors compromise learning, the teacher's job becomes more difficult. Of course, have college students ever been easy to teach? Perhaps more of them were when only the brightest and best came to college, but today, some sort of post-secondary education is an option for everyone. Many students now arrive without skills essential to success in most post-secondary environments. They write poorly, struggle to calculate math, aren't able to read college-level materials, and don't have good study skills. Add to that their willingness to engage in behaviors known to compromise learning: they don't come to class or show up unprepared. They procrastinate, waiting until the last minute to write papers and study for exams. And they pretty much all believe that multitasking while they study has no negative consequences.

You will still hear mumblings on campus about how students this poorly prepared shouldn't be in college and that it isn't our job to teach basic skills, but these students have been admitted by the institution and that if they graduate from college poorly prepared for the workplace, the teaching-basic-skills-isn't-our-job excuse won't win us any points.

Fortunately, resources that teachers can use to help students develop these missing skills abound. There's a healthy sample in this collection and lots more where these came from.

And here's something helpful to remember: don't assume you have to remediate every missing basic skill and ineffective approach to learning. You don't have to do it all; we're in this together. It's better to identify the skills necessary for success, given your course content and assignments, and then work with students on those skills.

Missing basic skills

Note-Taking: A Helpful Handout for Students

Reason to read: Students should be taking notes for themselves. Many don't want to, don't like to, and don't take good notes. One answer: give them yours, which causes many students to smile, but your notes make sense to you and students need notes meaningful to them. The better answer: work with them on their note-taking skills.

Should I recopy my notes after class? No, because recopying requires little or no thinking. Your time could be better spent writing questions and answers about the material in your notes.

Should I record the lecture?

Generally, no. Relistening takes a lot of time and in most cases, other, less time-consuming ways of reviewing and organizing the material are just as effective. The only possible exception here might involve students for whom English is not the primary language. For these students, relistening aids comprehension and improves language skills.

Should I try to listen and not write when the instructor is discussing something I don't understand?

No, the best advice is to keep taking notes. Leave blank spaces if you are missing content and question marks to indicate that you are just copying something down but don't really understand what it means. Most instructors would happily entertain a question whenever something is unclear. If you don't ask then, review your notes later and see if another student can help you understand this material or ask your instructor to re-explain it to you then.

What should I do if the professor talks so fast, I can't get everything written down?

Are you trying to write down everything the professor says word for word? Try not to do that—paraphrase, listen for the most important things the professor says, and leave blank spaces to indicate that you have missed some material you thought was important. Check a classmate's notes to see if they got the material down.

What should I do if my mind is always wandering while the professor is talking?

Sit in the front of the room. Being close to the professor helps students pay attention. Ask a question. If your mind wanders away, make it a short side trip. Get back to what's happening in class quickly. Try paying really close attention to those parts of the lecture that are most important. When does the instructor convey the most important material? Make sure that you are paying attention then.

How do I deal with an instructor who constantly wanders off the topic?

Can you pick out the important principles? Does the professor structure the material so that it makes sense and logically hangs together? In situations like these, it really helps to work with other students. Form a small study group and spend time organizing notes from class. What does everyone think the most important ideas were? How does one idea relate to another?

Sometimes the instructor uses words I don't know how to spell. What should I do?

Write the words as they sound. Follow the word with the notation "sp?" which should signal you when reviewing that you need to find out (from a fellow classmate, the text, or a dictionary) how to spell a word.

Adapted from: Dembo, M. H. (2000). *Motivation and Learning Strategies for College Success: A Self-Management Approach.* Mahwah, NJ: Lawrence Erlbaum, 176–77.

Reprinted from *The Teaching Professor,* Nov 2003

Recommended Resource

Cohan, D., Kim, E., Tan, J., and Winkelmes, M., (2013). A note-restructuring intervention increases students' exam scores. *College Teaching,* 61 (Summer), 95–99.

This article offers a creative assignment that gets students reformatting content in their notes in ways that develop note-taking skills and that resulted in more correct answers to test questions covering that content.

Reading Prompts

Reason to read: Many students don't have college-level reading skills, and not having them can seriously hinder learning in college and beyond. It's possible to develop reading assignments that get students doing the reading and that simultaneously develop those nascent reading skills. Here's a set of reading prompts that directs and deepens student thinking via a flexible assignment that doesn't take hours to grade.

Students can critically read in a variety of ways:

- When they raise vital questions and problems from the text,
- When they gather and assess relevant information and then offer plausible interpretations of that information,
- When they test their interpretations against previous knowledge or experience...,
- When they examine their assumptions and the implications of those assumptions, and
- When they use what they have read to communicate effectively with others or to develop potential solutions to complex problems." (p. 127)

And don't we all wish our students read this way! Unfortunately, most of them don't, and the challenge is finding those strategies and approaches that help them develop these sophisticated reading skills. Terry Tomasek, who crafted this description of critical reading, proposes one such strategy: she uses reading prompts. "The purpose of these reading/writing prompts is to facilitate personal connection between the undergraduate student and the assigned text. The prompts are simply questions used to orient students with a critical reading stance and to guide their thinking as they read." (p. 128) Her goal in using the prompts is to help students identify the big ideas, rather than just "mining" the text for facts and details. She's not against facts and details, but she thinks that's what a lot of students look for when they read. In contrast, the big ideas are what prompt the reflection and analysis typical of those who read deeply and think critically.

Tomasek uses prompts that promote a range of critical thinking responses. The categorization she has developed is neither linear nor hierarchical, which means the prompts can be used in any order. Here's her six categories and a selection of sample prompts.

Identification of problem or issue
- What problem is the author identifying? Who does the problem relate to?
- For whom is this topic important and why?

Making connections
- How is what I am reading different from what I already know? Why might this difference exist?
- What new ideas are here for me to consider? Why am I willing or not willing to consider them.

Interpretation of evidence
- What inferences can I make from the evidence given in the reading sample?
- What relevant evidence or examples does the author give to support his or her justification?

Challenging assumptions
- What kind of assumptions is the author making? Do I share these assumptions?
- What information builds my confidence in the author's expertise?
- If the opportunity arose, what questions would I pose to the author?

Making application
- What advice could I add to this reading selection? On what basis do I give this advice?
- Looking toward where I want to be in two years, what suggestions from the reading make the most sense to me?

Taking a different point of view
- What would I point out as important about this topic to others who either question or disagree with my point of view?

As for the mechanics, Tomasek assigns one reading prompt when the reading assignment is made. Students respond in one or two paragraphs prior to the next class. They are asked to share their responses to the prompts in a variety of ways. They might post them on a Blackboard discussion space and then respond to the comments posted by other classmates. This electronic exchange takes place before class. Tomasek may use material from these exchanges when she discusses the reading in class. Other times, students e-mail their response to another student, who then asks clarifying questions when they meet face-to-face at the beginning of class. Or students may simply write out their responses to the prompt and e-mail it to the instructor, who uses them in a variety of ways as the content is presented and discussed in class.

Tomasek instructs students not to worry about grammar, punctuation, or paragraph structure in their responses. What students are being asked to prepare is not a writing assignment, but an attempt to help them uncover the big ideas, to see how they relate and can be applied. When students submit their responses, the feedback provided is limited and the papers are not graded. However, Tomasek does keep track of student responses, making sure that they are doing the reading and responding thoughtfully.

Reference: Tomasek, T. (2009). Critical reading: Using reading prompts to promote active engagement with text. *International Journal of Teaching and Learning in Higher Education*, 21(1), 127–132.

Condensed and revised version of an article from *The Teaching Professor*, Dec 2010

Reading Groups Get Students Reading

Reason to read: Don't underestimate the power of peer pressure. Students can be motivated to do their reading if they have to talk about it with their classmates. No, they aren't going to just sit around and engage in academic discourse on their own; they need a specific task. Here's an example which has design features that make the most of peer pressure.

This strategy was developed by two sociologists; they report on their experiences using it in 12 different sections of four different courses and at three different institutions. Students in these courses are assigned individual readings, as opposed to a textbook, often on "highly politicized subject matter" (p. 364) like race and gender. The reading groups, each with five or six members, are formed by the teacher, who works to create diverse groups so that students are more likely to hear various viewpoints. Students complete an information survey at the beginning of the course which is used to form the groups.

Group reading discussions take place in class on dates specified in the course calendar. Students arrive in class having done readings and with a completed reading preparation sheet. In general, they are allotted 20 to 30 minutes for their discussions, although in some courses, discussion times were longer.

One of the interesting design features of this assignment are the roles students are assigned: *discussion leader, passage master, creative connector, devil's advocate,* and *reporter*. Students assume one of these roles in each discussion, but not the same role each time. The discussion leader comes to the discussion with prepared questions (and brief answers) that he or she uses to facilitate the discussion. The *passage master* brings several important passages—ones that provide key information. They may be controversial, or just a passage the passage master finds interesting. He or she is prepared to summarize these passages for the group. The *creative connector* makes connections between the readings and other "social, cultural, political, or economic ideas." (p. 357) They may be connections to other readings or they may be advertisements, clips from YouTube, cartoons, or references to movie content. The *devil's advocate* prepares a list of questions raised by critics of the authors or by those whose viewpoints differ. The *reporter* summarizes the group's discussion, including topics upon which they agreed and disagreed, points of confusion, and ideas the group found most interesting. These roles are described on a handout given to students, which is included in an appendix at the end of the article. Students rotate through the roles during the course.

Participation in these group reading discussions counts for between 10 and 30 percent of the course grade. Students are graded individually, not as a group, and their grade is based on their reading preparation sheets as well as a peer assessment of their participation in the group. Reading preparation sheets may be turned in on discussion days, posted electronically, or retained and submitted at the end of the course in a reading portfolio. The authors have used all these strategies and report the assets and liabilities of each. They are also considering having students review all their reading preparation sheets before turning them in and then writing a paper in which they reflect on their reading and reading discussion experiences.

Student responses to this strategy have been very positive. Data reported in the article shows that on a 5-point scale with 5 being always, the "how often did you complete the readings for this course" question received a 4.25 overall average. The average response to the "were the actual reading groups/class meetings helpful for understanding the readings" question, again with 5 being always, was 4.35, and a question about whether the prep sheets and discussion helped students see connections between the readings and everyday life garnered an overall average of 4.43.

This is a useful article with various handout materials appended and all the logistical details carefully described. The authors correctly conclude, "The group format described here can provide the basis for collaborative learning within a range of courses within and beyond sociology." (p. 365)

Reference: Parrott, H. M., and Cherry, E. (2011). Using structured reading groups to facilitate deep learning. *Teaching Sociology*, 39(4), 354–370.

Condensed and revised version of an article from *The Teaching Professor,* Jan 2012

Behaviors that compromise learning

Excuses, Excuses, Excuses

Reason to read: You don't have to teach for very long before it feels like you've heard every excuse in the book, and sorting out the legitimate ones from those that are made up can be frustrating and time-consuming. It's good to have a big-picture plan like the one provided here.

"Grandpa's heart exploded, but he's fine now," one student reported the morning after missing a scheduled exam. "I caught dyslexia from another student last semester," responded another when his teacher asked him about all the spelling mistakes in his paper. And then there was the pet rabbit that swallowed a needle on the day of the big group presentation. Excuses like these are so preposterous they can't help but make us laugh, but dealing with them is no laughing matter.

As a recent book for new psychology teachers points out, "The way you handle excuses conveys a message to your students about your teaching philosophy, and most particularly about whether you view students as partners or adversaries, the degree to which you trust them, and how you care about them." (p. 137)

Some faculty opt for the hard line: no excuses accepted, none, under any terms. That was my policy early on. Then one semester a responsible, dedicated student lost his father in a car accident. He missed the exam to attend the funeral. In a situation like that, the hard line policy fails pitifully.

On the other hand, it does seem absolutely true that the more excuses you accept, the more you are asked to consider. You can err on the side of gullibility, but learning that an excuse placates for missed deadlines, scheduled presentations, and far-in-advance exam dates should not be the lesson reinforced by experiences in college.

And so the teacher must adjudicate with firmness and with finesse. I'd like to report that it gets easier with age. It doesn't. Some students are very good at making up stories and some with legitimate excuses don't present them very persuasively. The net result: sometimes even concerned and caring teachers make mistakes. If they can be rectified, fine; if not, life does go on.

As for a general rule of thumb, authors of the book referenced here recommend "taking a firm, consistent, rational, and caring approach to excuses that incorporates a 'trust, but verify' policy. Treat every excuse as genuine, but in fairness to the entire class, require that it be verified, accompanied by supporting documentation." (p. 137).

Reference: Lucas, S. G. and Bernstein, D. A. (2005). *Teaching Psychology: A Step by Step Guide*. Mahweh, NJ: Lawrence Erlbaum.

A condensed and revised version of an article from *The Teaching Professor*, Jan 2006

Something to think about...

Here's the scenario: an assignment worth 5 percent of the grade is due in class in an hour. Alex realizes he's not going to get it done before class. A cohort of 316 students were asked what they would do if they were in Alex's shoes. A full 60 percent reported they would make up an excuse and use it to justify asking for more time.

Reference: Carmichael, A. M., & Carmichael, L. E. (2014). An examination of factors and attitudes that influence fraudulent claim in an academic environment. Active Learning in Higher Education, 15(2), 173–185.

Cramming for Exams

Reason to read: Why do students cram for exams? Because they always have? Yes, but the answer is a bit more in-your-face. They cram because it works, more often than you might imagine.

Do students cram for your exams? Maybe the answers depends on how cramming is defined. How about this definition from a 1968 study: cramming is "a period of neglect of study followed by a concentrated burst of studying immediately before an exam." (p. 227)

It will probably not shock any instructor to learn that research verifies the continued use of cramming. What may be a bit surprising is the number of students who do: somewhere between about 25 percent and 50 percent, depending on the study. In the research reported in the article referenced here, about 45 percent of students were on the "agree" side of a scale measuring the extent of cramming.

Here's what is definitely surprising: cramming as a study strategy is effective, at least by some criteria. This article's literature review section lists five different studies conducted between 1968 and 2001; all of them found that cramming did not negatively affect course grades. Instead, it found more mixed results. If students agreed that they used cramming "for most of my courses," those students tended to have a lower GPA; the opposite was also true. However, this study looked at a particular course, Principles of Marketing, and for that course, "the course grade is not significantly related to the degree of cramming reportedly used in the course." (p. 233)

The problem with cramming has to do with retention and here, previous research (including this study) offers conclusive results. When students cram, the information is stored in short-term memory, and information stored there doesn't stay long. The results reported in this study illustrate this finding in a very graphic way. A student in the "high cramming" category with a course grade of 85 would, at 150 weeks after the course (based on predictions derived from repeated test scores), retain only 27 percent of what he or she learned in the course. Several different models are used to project the progression of this "learning decay." Results are equally bleak in all cases.

Interestingly, it is not a case of one testing format promoting more cramming than another. Researchers worried that perhaps multiple-choice testing methods actually encouraged cramming. That hypothesis was not confirmed by their results. Students crammed just as often for essay exams as they did for multiple-choice exams.

There is some cause for optimism, though. Students in this study "resoundingly agree" that cramming is not a strategy that enhances long-term learning and retention. They know it's not the way to really learn the material. But because so many of their peers study this way, because college students tend to procrastinate, because they lead busy lives, and because it often generates decent (if not good) grades, cramming is an appealing alternative.

This is another one of those articles packed full of good information on an important topic. It includes the 49-question instrument developed to determine if students crammed and if they thought the approach was effective. Administering an instrument like this to students can be as revealing to them as to the instructor.

Teachers are taken to task for their teaching methods by the study's researchers. "The all-too-common use of PowerPoint slide lectures, even with in-class handouts of the slides, does not engage students to take notes in their own language and handwriting, which shunts the processing of the material, leaving all effective learning to the cramming period at the end of the term." (p. 237) In other words, it's not just test formats that assess deep learning that forestall cramming—how material is presented in class can also make a difference.

Reference: McIntyre, S. H. & Munson, J. M. (2008). Exploring cramming: Student behaviors, beliefs, and learning retention in the Principles of Marketing course. *Journal of Marketing*, 30(3), 226–243.

A condensed and revised version of an article from *The Teaching Professor,* Jan 2009

Multitasking: It Doesn't Mix Well with Learning

Reason to read: How do we get students to realize that multitasking has consequences for learning? Telling them isn't convincing. Would evidence be more persuasive?

Evidence that multitasking and learning don't mix continues to grow. The article referenced below cites numerous studies reporting negative relationships between technology multitasking and learning. This should concern teachers, given how many students are avid technology users. Students in this study were taking courses at institutions where the average class size was a bit less than 23. Even with these comparatively small classes, 50 percent of the students said they were frequently text messaging in class. Twenty-five percent reported frequently checking Facebook while in class.

To document the frequency of multitasking, the researcher of this study surveyed 774 students. Only 5.6 percent reported no multitasking behaviors in class. More than 50 percent of the students indicated that they were text messaging in class frequently or very frequently; almost 25 percent said the same for checking Facebook. Many students at this institution take online courses and the extent of multitasking they reported during those courses was even higher. Almost 63 percent reported checking Facebook, almost 70 percent said they were text messaging, and almost 67 percent said they were listening to music.

The relationship between multitasking and grades was significant: "... the more multitasking a person engaged in, the lower his or her overall grade," (p. 7) said the study author. Moreover, this analysis also documented a negative relationship between multitasking and a series of high-risk behaviors. "Individuals with higher multitasking scores drank significantly more alcohol, smoked more cigarettes, used more marijuana and…'other' drugs than those with lower scores. High multitaskers were also significantly more likely to have engaged in binge drinking, driven a car after drinking alcohol, being driven in a car by someone who has drunk alcohol, gotten into physical fights, and had multiple sex partners in the past 30 days than lower multitaskers." (p. 7)

The researcher points out that, "although it is very likely that students have been engaging in distracting behaviors in the classroom throughout the history of education, the ubiquity of technologies seems to make the possibilities for classroom multitasking even more likely in the near future." (p. 9).

The question is what teachers should do about this problem. It seems like the place to start is with students. Many seem to think that they can multitask with no negative consequences. They need to be confronted with evidence that disavows this conclusion. The article cites a number of studies with very specific results: lower scores on a quiz taken after a lecture during which students were allowed to text message; taking between 22 and 59 percent more time to complete a reading assignment when used instant messaging (IM) while reading (not counting the time spent sending messages); and lower GPAs and less time spent studying for Facebook users. Student may continue multitasking, but they should do so knowing that there are consequences to that decision.

Should teachers confront students? Should laptops, cell phones, and other devices be banned in the classroom? Doing so can meet with fierce student resistance and require devoting lots of time and effort to enforcing such a policy. Alternatively, teachers are devising ways of harnessing these technology options to learning. That seems like a promising solution. But when teachers avert their eyes and pretend multitasking isn't happening, they ignore behaviors known to compromise learning outcomes and that does seem like an abrogation of instructional responsibility.

Reference: Burak, L. (2012). Multitasking in the university classroom. *International Journal for the Scholarship of Teaching and Learning.* 6(2).

Revised version of an article published in *The Teaching Professor*, Oct 2012

Metacognitive Pestering for Beginning Students

by Matt Birkenhauer, Northern Kentucky University, birkenhauer@nku.edu

Reason to read: When students are missing basic skills and engaging in behaviors that compromise their learning experiences, what else can we do? Here's a suggestion.

Watching my own son spend his first semester in college struggling with meeting deadlines was an "up close" reminder of something I have learned after 30 years of teaching. Beginning college students are often spacey. They have lots on their minds and need help in that commonplace of contemporary pedagogy called metacognitive thinking.

Most of us know what metacognitive thinking is. John Flavell, the psychologist who coined the term in the late 1970s, defines it as "one's knowledge concerning one's own cognitive processes and products or anything related to them—for example, learning relevant properties or information or data." More simply, it can be described as "thinking about one's own thinking" or, as a colleague of mine likes to say, "making thinking visible."

How can college teachers "make thinking visible" for harried, busy, and not always terribly mature freshmen who don't just take classes but work, date, and attempt to skirt the dividing line between studying and partying? One way is to pester them—be "helicopter instructors," at least to some extent. Now, I do agree wholeheartedly with those who warn against the dangers of helicopter parents. But I don't think it's the same when college teachers work to clarify the demands and culture of higher education for beginning students. Many are first-generation college students and need mentors to "hover" around them in those first college courses.

I think a lot of us already do this. Thankfully, several of my son's instructors had these kinds of conversations with him as he was foundering in his first semester. I do it in my introductory writing classes by using Blackboard to pester my students. For example, many of them used "cram writing" to get through four years of high school (despite the best efforts of their hard-working teachers). I start talking about cram writing in class the first two weeks of the semester. Then I reinforce that message with an e-mail that I send out through Blackboard as the deadline for their first major writing assignment nears. If the assignment is due Tuesday, this is the note students receive on Saturday:

> If you want to write a quality essay, avoid what I call "cramming," which is about as effective in writing as it is in studying. What is cram writing? Cram writing is waiting until the night before the rough draft is due to begin writing. This causes you to write quickly and unthinkingly; it also denies you the opportunity to creatively reflect on what you wrote—to "chew" over it a bit.
>
> Today is Saturday. If you haven't done so yet, begin drafting an introduction today. Look at it for a few minutes before you go to bed tonight. Look at it again in the morning. Try to write another half or third of your essay tomorrow. Then think how much less work you'll have left to do by Tuesday.

I don't send out this e-mail out until I have provided the scaffolding students need to begin writing a rough draft: helping them determine what their theses are, allowing them to complete the research for their assignments, and having them plan in class the form their essays will take. But I follow this first "pestering" e-mail with others, some containing blunt reminders like this one: DON'T CRAM WRITE, DON'T CRAM WRITE, DON'T CRAM WRITE, which I repeat multiple times in the note.

Some of this "metacognitive pestering" is self-serving, in that the more students avoid cram writing, the more organized and clear their essays are. This makes my job of responding to their rough drafts easier.

This kind of "hovering," aimed at making students think about when and how they are completing their assignments, doesn't work at all if students aren't getting the message. Early in the course, I offer reminders about the importance of these class-related communications. I'm not recommending this approach for students at all levels. But I do think beginning students benefit when their teachers intervene with the kind of advice and reminders that set in place successful approaches to learning.

Reprinted from *The Teaching Professor,* Apr 2010

A primer on learning

Introduction

Interest in learning abounds in higher education, and that interest is long overdue. Various disciplines have been studying learning for decades and what they've discovered (information with great relevance to teachers) is finally making its way into mainstream pedagogical literature.

Unfortunately, a lot of what's known about learning only serves to underscore its complexity. Learning can be described as a simple process. However, it's anything but simple when it occurs. The place to start is with some grounding principles, which are the first step in developing evidence-based teaching practices. Resources here will get you started and also point the way to other good resources. Moreover, the information here is good material to share with students who don't usually know much about learning or about themselves as learners.

Learning: Five Key Principles

Reason to read: Any short summary of what's known about learning flies high above a large knowledge domain, but short summaries like this one are a good way to at least get the lay of the land.

A review of the research on active learning compiled for physiology faculty contains five "key findings" that author Joel Michael maintains ought "to be incorporated in our thinking as we make decisions about teaching physiology (I would say, name your discipline) at any educational level." (p. 160) Here's the list, along with a brief discussion of each.

Learning involves the active construction of meaning by the learner. This well-established principle involves the fact that students link new information to information they already know. New and old information combines to form mental models. If the old information is faulty, that compromises the learning of new information. "Learning can be thought about as a process of conceptual change in which faulty or incomplete models are repaired." (p. 161) Fixing faulty mental models can be very difficult, as witnessed by research documenting that even after taking a course on a particular topic (physics is often used as an example), students may still hold serious misconceptions about it.

Learning facts and learning to do something are two different processes. This explains why students can know a set of facts and still be unable to apply those facts to solve a problem. If students are to successfully use knowledge, they must have opportunities to practice and obtain feedback. A variety of other instructional advice follows from this principle, including the fact that students who are learning to solve problems need to know more than whether the answer is right or wrong. How problems move in sequence from easy to hard also has consequences for learning. Students should only move to harder problems as they improve. Moving them too quickly often compromises their efforts to learn.

Some things that are learned are specific to the domain or context (subject matter or course) in which they were learned, whereas other things are more readily transferred to other domains. What's at issue here is knowledge transfer and whether students can take what they know about one subject or topic and transfer that knowledge to another subject or topic. As many college teachers have observed, students often have great trouble with this. There are still a number of research controversies in this area, but there is growing recognition that transfer involves skills that students need to be taught.

Individuals are likely to learn more when they learn with others than when they learn alone. Many faculty are very independent learners and so struggle a bit with accepting this principle. However, it is based on "impressive results" in different disciplines "that support the power of getting students to work together to learn." (p. 162)

Meaningful learning is facilitated by articulating explanations, whether to one's self, peers, or teachers. Students learn to speak the languages of disciplines when they practice speaking those languages. That's part of what this principle involves, but it is also true that articulating an answer, an idea, or a level of understanding aids in learning. Speaking or writing makes clear to learners what they do and don't understand, and their understanding deepens as they frame a description that is meaningful to them.

Like any set of principles, these are general statements that, in this case, cover large, complex research areas. They are a useful means of getting a broad perspective. Decisions about instructional practices can certainly be based upon these principles; however, one should not read the principles and assume an in-depth understanding of the complicated phenomenon called learning.

Reference: Michael, J. (2006). Where's the evidence that active learning works? Advances in Physiology Education, 30, 159–167.

A slightly revised version of the original, reprinted from *The Teaching Professor,* Mar 2011

Metacognition: Three Ways Students Can Learn about Learning

Reason to read: Students need to know more about learning in general and themselves as learners specifically. Here's a set of suggestions for teachers interested in developing students as learners.

Metacognition is about being able to successfully plan, monitor, and evaluate your learning. It's not a skill that can be listed as a strength of most of our students. Few have encountered themselves as learners. They don't have an expansive repertoire of study strategies. They don't often think about alternatives when the studying isn't going all that well. And most don't evaluate how well they learned beyond the grade they receive. It's something else concerned teachers need to worry about teaching students.

Kimberly Tanner thinks we can help students become more metacognitively aware by building classroom cultures "grounded in metacognition." (p. 116) In other words, by creating a classroom climate that confronts students with themselves as learners. Tanner suggests three ways of doing so. Tanner writes specifically to biologists, but her points are true of most college classrooms.

Encourage students to express their confusion in class. "While most faculty welcome questions from students in or out of class, it is generally not in the culture of college science courses for students to share their confusions; rather, there is a focus on right answers and on being scientifically correct." (p. 117)

Alternatively, students could be encouraged to ask themselves what they don't understand and then express those areas in class (or online) to their benefit, as well as to the benefit of other students and the teacher. Sometimes what students describe as confusing causes confusion for the teacher, probably because she understands the area so well, but that's an instance where students can often help each other or the teacher understand what it is they don't understand. In the same vein, students can be encouraged to ask each other about what they don't understand. Or the teacher can identify what has confused former students about this concept. The goal here is simply to make it acceptable to say in class and to other learners, "I don't understand."

Make reflection a part of graded course work. If students are answering questions about assigned reading or submitting homework problems, they can be asked various questions: "Were any ideas in the reading confusing, challenging, difficult to understand, or ideas you'd never considered previously?" "Which homework problem was the most difficult? What made it difficult?" "If you got stuck on a problem but finally figured it out, what helped you get to the solution?" As long as students are making a good-faith effort to answer these questions, they can receive full credit. The value of questions like these is the metacognitive thinking they stimulate.

Think out loud in front of students. In other words, model "how you start, how you decide what to do first and then next, how you check your work, how you know when you are done." (p. 118)

Can you recall when you first learned the concept you are trying to teach? Was it confusing? Share with students what confused you and how you found your way to understanding. Obviously, examples based on course content are most relevant, but teachers can demonstrate metacognition with any learning tasks. Are you stuck on something in your research? How are you trying to figure it out? What resources and colleagues are you consulting? How many solutions have you tried so far that haven't worked? As many who teach writing know, students think revising is only necessary if you didn't get it right the first time. They are surprised to see a piece of their teacher's writing that has been revised and to learn that the changes are not just one set of revisions, but five different attempts to make the writing better.

Tanner makes one last point worth mentioning. The call for more active learning has been heard and many teachers are working diligently to get students active and engaged in class. Kudos to every teacher who is trying to give students the opportunity to learn by doing. However, as Tanner notes, students can be active, including doing a hands-on activity, but they can be doing it and still not be doing much thinking. Activity in and of itself does not promote learning. Activity must be accompanied with a metacognitive component that requires students to process what they doing, why they are

doing it, and what they are learning from doing it.
Reference: Tanner, K. D. (2012). Promoting student metacognition. *Cell Biology Education—Life Sciences Education,* 11 (Summer), 113–120.

A revised version of the original, reprinted from *The Teaching Professor,* Nov 2012

Recommended Resource
Benassi, V. A., Overson, C. E., & Hakala, C. M. (eds.). (2014). Applying science of learning in education: Infusing psychological science into the curriculum. Retrieved from the Society for the Teaching of Psychology website: http://teachpsych.org/ebooks/asle2014/index.php
An amazing free resource with chapters summarizing much of the current research on learning, many authored by those doing the research. The writing is accessible and most chapters include suggestions for implementing what the research has established.

Understanding motivation

Introduction

Getting students who'd rather be passive engaged begins by understanding the powerful role motivation plays in learning. Unfortunately, a lot of students don't seem all that motivated to learn, especially in courses they're required to take. They'd rather sit back and have education done unto them, preferably via a painless process. The most common teacher response to absent motivation is the proverbial stick—extrinsic motivation. It does get most students doing what they need to do, but not because they want to. They're in class because attendance is graded. Their papers come in on time because they lose points if they're late. But what extrinsic motivation can accomplish, intrinsic motivation thoroughly trumps. It motivates learning for the right reasons. Education would improve significantly if teachers relied less on extrinsic and worked harder at promoting intrinsic motivation. The research is helpful here: a lot is known about motivates learners and much of it can be applied in our courses.

Most teachers seek to engage students via participation. However, despite widespread use, participation is not all that successful an engagement strategy. Research regularly documents that only about 50 percent of students participate and that a few tend to over-participate, offering as much as 80 percent of the comments made in a course. Despite commitments to participation, many faculty still talk most of the time, even during most of the time when they are interacting with students. There are lots of issues here, but also lots of solutions, and many of them are easy to implement once we start paying attention to how participation is (or isn't) working in our courses. **More and better participation** is an option in every course.

The basic justification for using group work rests on the well-documented fact that students can learn from and with each other. They don't do so automatically, just because they are assembled in a group by the teacher. There are **keys to successful group work** that start with how the groups are formed, what tasks they are given to complete, how the group functions, and how group learning is assessed. Groups are being used by faculty in virtually every discipline, so there is a rich pool of resources available.

Understanding Student Motivation

Reason to read: Here's the essence of a 20-page review of research compiled by one of the most prominent researchers on student motivation. It's a nutshell introduction to one of the essentials of effective instruction.

What motivates students in classrooms? It's one of those $64,000 questions—of interest because we so often see students in classrooms who aren't motivated. They look bored, apathetic, there because they have to be, sitting back and waiting for education to be done unto them. To be sure, these descriptors don't apply to all college students, but most of us would agree that they characterize far too many of the learners that sit in front of us.

The question with which we opened is not only one being asked by faculty practitioners, it is a research question which, over the years, has generated much theory and empirical inquiry. For the past several decades, one of the most prominent names in motivation research, especially at the college level, has been Paul Pintrich of the University of Michigan. Shortly before his untimely death in 2003, he completed a comprehensive, exceptionally well organized, and amazingly accessible review of research on motivation as it relates to teaching and learning contexts. He organizes what is known around seven key questions, one of those being the question with which we opened. His response to each question involves five generalizations or conclusions, each drawn from different streams of theory and research. Especially noteworthy are the design principles he extrapolates from each. They are his attempt to not only answer the question but to translate research findings into principles faculty can apply in the design of classroom policies and practices.

Here are those generalizations, briefly discussed, with a sample of the recommended design principles.

Adaptive self-efficacy and competence perceptions motivate students. Research terminology is included in the review, but it is almost always translated, as in the case of this generalization. "Students who believe that they are able and that they can and will do well are much more likely to be motivated in terms of effort, persistence, and behavior than students who believe they are less able and do not expect to succeed." (p. 671) Much research stands behind this principle, a lot of it referenced in the article. Pintrich includes many important details, like how accurate students' perceptions are and if they are able to adapt or change their perceptions in response to feedback. Pintrich suggests two design principles:

1) **Provide clear and accurate feedback regarding competence and self-efficacy, focusing on the development of competence, expertise, and skill.** This is especially important in the case of students who don't believe strongly in their abilities: they need to have their progress pointed out.

2) **Design tasks (like activities and assignment) that offer opportunities to be successful but also challenge students.** The principle is sometimes difficult to realize in practice, but tasks that are too hard or too easy de-motivate students.

Adaptive attributions and control beliefs motivate students. "The basic construct refers to beliefs about the causes of success and failure and how much perceived control one has to bring about outcomes or to control one's behavior." (p. 673) Obviously, this principle relates to the first one, but the emphasis here is on situations in which the learning occurs and the student's beliefs about his or her ability to control the outcome. If the student comes to class, does the homework, and thoroughly prepares for the exam, will that produce a high exam score? If a student doesn't think effort makes a difference, he or she won't expend any. The design principles then propose that faculty **provide feedback that stresses [the] process nature of learning, including the importance of effort, strategies, and potential self-control of learning.** And secondly, student motivation will be positively impacted if faculty **provide students with opportunities to exercise some choice and control.**

Higher levels of interest and intrinsic motivation motivate students. Research here makes an important distinction between personal and situational interest. Personal interest "represents an individual's relatively enduring disposition to be attracted to, to enjoy, or to like to be engaged in a particularly activity or topic." (p. 674) Our choice of discipline often reflects that interest and explains why student motivation is a less of a problem in upper-division major courses. Situational interest refers to "being interested in a task or activity that is generated by the interestingness of the task or context." (p. 674) The design principle is easy to guess and should perhaps be the mantra for those entry-level required courses not of interest to students: **Provide stimulating and interesting tasks, activities, and materials, including some novelty and variety in tasks and activities.** Students frequently discover new interests in college, and they often do because faculty **display and model interest and involvement in the content and activities.**

Higher levels of value motivate students. In addition to how interested students are in the subject and the task, it also "matters whether students care about or think the task is important in some way." (p. 675) For example, research here documents that if students think a course is likely to equip them with important, valuable skills or content, they are more likely to enroll in that course. Among a couple of design principles proposed here, Pintrich recommends that **classroom discourse should focus on [the] importance and utility of content and activities.**

Goals motivate and direct students. Research here has gone in several different directions, and some of it has ended up with very specific outcomes, like a taxonomy of 24 goals individuals might pursue generally which have been studied specifically in the classroom context. Of special note is research substantiating that students are not only motivated by academic goals but also by social ones. Pintrich notes that this research on social goals "highlights the importance of peer groups and interactions with other students as important contexts for the shaping and development of motivation, a context that has tended to be ignored...." (p. 675) Work on mastery and performance goals has also occurred in this area. The design principles that pertain to social and academic goals propose that faculty **use cooperative and collaborative groups to allow for opportunities to attain both social and academic goals.**

It is impossible to read a review like this and not be impressed by how much work has been done on motivation—much of it relevant, useful, and applicable in classroom contexts. It is also causes some chagrin to realize how much of it is unknown to faculty. Rarely do our discussions of motivation have this sort of depth and detail. And so this conclusion contains another admonition: if you've never read a review of research piece on an educational topic, I can't think of a finer place to start. If you've got some colleagues interested in upping the ante with respect to instructional discourse, discussion of this piece would do that.

What motivates students in classrooms? Lots of things, many of which we don't take advantage of in our educational practice.

Reference: Pintrich, P. R. (2003). A motivational science perspective on the role of student motivation in learning and teaching contexts. Journal of Educational Psychology, 95(4), 667–686.

Reprinted from *The Teaching Professor,* Mar 2004

More and better participation

Reasons Why Students Do or Don't Participate

Reason to read: Using participation to engage more students in learning starts with a clear understanding of what motivates students who do and don't participate. Here's a good run-down of those reasons.

Here's something many scholars no longer even attempt: a multi-disciplinary review of the literature, in this case on in-class participation. Author Kelly A. Rocca looked at articles on the topic published in academic journals between 1958 and 2009. The seven-page bibliography at the end of the review contains references including empirical studies, faculty reports involving their experiences using a particular kind of participation policy (some with data, some without), advice-giving articles, other literature reviews, and miscellaneous reports. It's an impressive collection which attests to amount of work done on this instructional practice.

Based on this literature review, Rocca identifies five factors which influence whether or not a student decides to participate in class. What follows here is a short discussion of each.

Logistics. This principally involves class size. There is a good bit of research documenting that students are more willing to participate, less anxious about participating, and less able to hide in smaller classes. Some of the literature reviewed proposes ways in which participation can be encouraged in larger classes. Also discussed here are the implications of various policies on participation, with the bottom line being that if participation counts in the grading scheme, students are motivated to contribute more often.

Confidence and classroom apprehension. Some students do not participate because they feel intimated by their fellow classmates and by the instructor. This is particularly problematic in classrooms where a small percentage of the students are doing most of the participation. Unfortunately, that describes participation in many classrooms, according to a number of different studies. Sometimes students begin to participate once they feel comfortable with their classmates. Participation is also more likely when students are well-prepared, which can be encouraged by having them bring written answers to class or by talking about possible answers with a classmate before offering an answer to the whole class.

Personality traits. There is some evidence that traits like low self-esteem and a lack of assertiveness negatively influence a student's willingness to participate.

Instructor and classroom climate. Not surprising, instructors play an important role in participation decisions. The instructor behaviors that discourage participation include: not paying attention to students; making fun of them or putting them down; being overly critical; using lots of sarcasm, being overly opinionated; and being moody and unfriendly. When students and the teacher respect each other and when teachers communicate care and concern for students, there is a positive impact on how comfortable students feel, which adds to their confidence and increases levels of participation. There's lots of advice in the literature on creating these sorts of classroom climates such as knowing students' names, providing verbal and nonverbal feedback, and being a good listener. Even something as simple as making sure there is sufficient "wait time" after asking a question can build a climate that encourages participation.

Sex differences. In the early 1980s, evidence emerged that women were participating less in classrooms than men. Subsequent research explored a variety of gender conditions including the teacher's gender and whether the majority of students in the class were the same or a different sex than the teacher. Results were mixed, but more recent research has found little evidence supportive of a "chilly classroom climate" for women students.

The literature reviewed here makes it clear that a student's decision to participate is not a simple one, but is instead determined by a confluence of factors. Some of those factors are beyond a teacher's ability to control, but many are not, and the literature referenced in this review offers considerable relevant research, ideas, and advice to those interested in promoting classroom participation.

Reference: Roccas, K. A. (2010). Student participation in the college classroom: An extended multidisciplinary literature review. *Communication Education,* 59(2), 185–213.

Reprinted from *The Teaching Professor,* May 2011

The Art of Asking Questions

Reason to read: Have you heard that old adage about quality questions getting quality answers? Could that be a recipe for more and better participation in our classrooms and online? Perhaps a thoughtful review of the questions you ask might be in order.

At one time or another, most of us have been disappointed by the caliber of the questions students ask in class, online, or in the office. Many of them are such mundane queries: "Will material from the book be on the exam?" "How long should the paper be?" "Can we use Google to find references?" "Would you repeat what you just said? I didn't get it all down in my notes." Rarely do they ask thoughtful questions that probe the content and stir the interest of the teacher and other students.

So how do we get them asking better questions? What if we try to start by asking our students the kind of questions we hope they will ask us? Here are some suggestions that might help us model what good questions are and demonstrate how instrumental they can be in promoting thinking, understanding, and learning.

Prepare questions. Too often, we ask questions as they come to us. Allen and Tanner write in an excellent article on questioning: "Although many teachers carefully plan test questions used as final assessments...much less time is invested in oral questions that are interwoven in our teaching." (p. 63) How many questions of the kind that generate discussion and lead to other questions come to us as we are teaching? Would more of those thought-provoking questions come to us if we thought about them as we prepare and contemplate the content for class?

Play with the question. Questions promote thinking before they are answered: it is in the interstices between the question and the answer that minds turn. In that time before answers happen, questions can be emphasized by having them on a PowerPoint or the board and by encouraging students to write the question in their notes. Maybe it's a question that opens class and doesn't get answered until the end of class. Maybe it's a question that gets asked repeatedly across several class sessions with any number of possible answers entertained before a "good" or "right" answer is designated.

Preserve good questions. If a question generates interest, thoughtful responses, and good discussion, that's a question to keep in some more permanent way than simply trying to remember it. Good questions can be preserved along with the course materials for that day. Finding them next semester enables us to revisit and possibly make them even better. Do we need to be reminded that probing questions about the content not only encourage students to think, but are good grist for the mill of our own thinking?

Ask questions that you don't know the answer to. Students tend to think that teachers have all the answers. Could that be because we answer all their questions? Marshall makes a point worth remembering. Typically, we ask students questions that we already know the answer to, and if any of you are like me, while the student is answering, you're quietly thinking how much better your answer is and how you will quickly deal with the student's answer so you can then give your own improved answer. Asking a question you don't know the answer to lets students know that you still have things to learn. Asking students those questions and then thoughtfully attending to their answers also indicates that you just might be able to learn something from a student. Could this be a way to motivate them to ask better questions?

Ask questions you can't answer. These questions are different from those you don't know the answer to. It's possible to find answers to those questions; *these* are the questions currently being confronted within the field or area of study that haven't yet been answered. As of this moment, the answers are unknown. A question that can't be answered is inherently more interesting than one that can be. Are there theories or research findings that suggest answers? Are some of those more likely than others? Could the answer be something totally unexpected? What if a student thinks he or she might have an idea about a possible answer?

Don't ask open-ended questions when you know the answer you're looking for. Sometimes students offer answers, but they aren't the ones the teacher wanted to hear. If you aren't getting the answer you want, don't play the "try to guess the answer I have in mind" game. It reinforces the idea that the question has one answer that the teacher thinks is the right or best answer. If the teacher has the answer, students are quick to conclude it's the definitive right response, and that makes it an answer that they won't spend any time thinking about.

We ask questions to get students interested, to help them understand, and to see if they do. We'd like for our questions to promote lively discussions during which thoughtful perspectives are exchanged, different views presented, and new ideas born. To accomplish that goal, we need to plan and use questions in more purposeful ways. If questions start playing a more prominent role in our teaching, the reward may be students asking questions we'd find interesting to answer and they'd find more interesting to discuss.

Shouldn't an article on questioning end with one? It should, and Allen and Tanner have a great one: "What would you predict would happen in your classroom if you changed the kinds of questions that you ask?" (p. 63)

References:

Allen, D., & Tanner, K. (2002). Approaches to cell biology teaching: Questions about questions. *Cell Biology Education*, 1, 63–67.

Marshall, G. (2006). From Shakespeare on the page to Shakespeare on the stage: What I learned about teaching in acting class. *Pedagogy*, 6(2), 309–325.

Reprinted from *The Teaching Professor,* Mar 2013

Something to think about...

"Hanging in the front office of the Research Academy for University Learning at Montclair State University is an old poster from the 1930s. It's one of those Depression-era placards encouraging schoolchildren to develop good habits. A little boy is tugging at a large yellow question mark, hooking a book labeled "knowledge." The caption reads: "Ask Questions. Sometimes the only way you can capture Mr. Knowledge is with a question mark." A bit stilted and old fashioned, the poster nevertheless captures something we've known for a long time: people are most likely to learn deeply when they are trying to answer their own questions or solve their own problems.

"Lots of evidence points to that conclusion. But here's the catch: in a formal educational environment, learners typically are not in charge of the questions. Teachers usually frame the curriculum and at least implicitly shape the questions."

Reference: Bain, K., & Zimmerman, J. (2009). Understanding great teaching. *Peer Review,* 11(2), 9–13.

Reprinted from The Teaching Professor blog, June 23, 2009

Ways of Responding to a Wrong or Not Very Good Answer

Reason to read: Teacher responses matter more when students give wrong or not very good answers. The stakes are higher when the mistake is made in front of others. It's good to have a repertoire of responses for those times when the answer is not very good or just plain wrong.

Whatever the relative quality of a student's response, teachers can respond in ways that increase the likelihood of participation by students in the future, or that result in fewer responses of a more questionable quality. For example, sometimes faculty will unintentionally demean or put down the student: "Where did you get that idea?" (asked in a tone of voice that makes the student think the idea is from outer space, even though the instructor is only trying to figure out how the student arrived at the answer).

Here's a collection of ways teachers can respond to wrong or not very good answers.

- Correct the answer. Fix it for the student and the rest of the class. Make it right.

- Get the class to correct or make the answer better. "Well, we need to work a bit more on Bob's answer. How would you make it stronger or better? What needs to be corrected?"

- Ask how the student arrived at that conclusion. "Explain your thinking." "Take us through the steps that led you to that conclusion."

- Defer to the rest of the class. "How many of you agree?" "How would you respond to this question?"

- Solicit a collection of answers before designating the right or best one. Let the class argue the merits of various answers on the way to identifying a good answer.

- Say that the answer is wrong, but don't make a big deal about it being wrong. Call it what it is and then move on to another student.

- "Here's the question you answered and that's not the question I asked." This response requires being able to quickly figure out what question the student answered, which is not always easy.

- Respond with positive feedback—don't say that the wrong answer is right, but offer feedback that lauds the effort. "No, but thanks for trying." "Close, but not quite right." "I'm glad you made that mistake—it a common one and now we get to correct it.

- Ask a follow-up question that leads the student to understand the error in the answer. "If that's correct, then how do you explain this?"

- Keep the focus on the answer. "This answer isn't very good" as opposed to "No, Mary, you're wrong."

- Try to find something in the answer that shows promise. This works fine in most humanities courses, but not in a math class.

The more challenging questions are: How do instructors know which strategy will work best, given the student who's just answered, the answer itself, and this particular class? How do instructors decide which strategy to use? Is it a conscious choice, or something more like a patterned response?

Reprinted from The Teaching Professor blog, May 13, 2008

Clickers: Taking a Look at the Research

Reason to read: Clickers, or classroom response systems, make participation a possibility for everyone. They are being used extensively in science courses and their use has generated a good deal of research with some interesting and persuasive results.

Here are highlights from one of those much needed and very useful cross-disciplinary reviews of research. Clickers, those classroom response systems that let students answer questions and get immediate feedback on their answers, are in wide use, and research exploring their effectiveness is being done in many disciplines. Shawn Keough's review looks at 66 studies undertaken in 16 different fields, "focusing on student perceptions/outcomes related to clicker use" (p. 824). The review does not include studies involving instructors: their attitudes, the reasons they do or don't use clickers, or their recommendations. Keough doesn't claim that this is a comprehensive review, but looking at this much research does provide a good overview—in this case, of what students are reporting about clickers. The article also includes a study of clicker use undertaken in a management setting. Those findings are consistent with conclusions drawn from the research review

The most obvious benefit of clickers is their provision of instantaneous feedback on student understanding. The teacher offers an explanation or uses an equation to solve a problem and then asks a question to see if students understand this new material. Before clickers, feedback could be obtained from one or two students; clickers now give teachers feedback from every student. With that feedback, it's easier for teachers to decide if they need to try a different explanation, do another problem, or home in on a particular area of misunderstanding. Beyond this benefit, Keough's review documents others as well. Here's a sample.

Improvement in classroom performance. The objective measures of improved performance used in the studies reviewed included exam scores, quiz scores, final grades, scores on pre- and posttests, mean pass rates, and standardized tests. Thirty-one of the studies involving 34 samples (each a different student cohort) included one or more of these measures, and 22 of those samples reported significant increases in those sections where clickers were being used. This improvement was based on comparing classes using clickers with comparable sections not using clickers. In 12 other samples, students did perform at higher levels, but those levels were not statistically significant. In 33 of the studies involving 37 samples, researchers asked students if they thought the use of clickers improved their performance in the course; students in 35 of those samples said that they did.

Increased student satisfaction. In 42 of the studies with 47 samples, high levels of student satisfaction were reported in 46 of the samples. These results were found via survey questions that asked things like whether clickers should continue to be used in future sections of the course.

Increased student attention and/or focus. Students in 23 of the studies with 25 samples were asked whether the use of clickers helped focus the class as a whole on the subject; students in 23 of the 25 samples said they did. Moreover, when asked to list some strengths of clicker systems, students regularly identified making it easier to pay attention as a benefit.

Improved attendance. Does the use of clickers improve student attendance? Twenty-four studies considered attendance; 19 of them reported that clickers did improve attendance. However, some of those studies measured better attendance by asking students if the use of clickers improved their attendance, whereas others graded attendance and measured it by clicker use during class. Removing these studies left nine where attendance in clicker classes was tracked and compared with attendance in classes not using clickers. Seven of those studies reported increased attendance in classes where clickers were used.

Improved participation. Nineteen studies with 21 samples examined how clickers affected participation. Again, the majority of the studies asked students how they thought the clickers affected their participation. Did they ask more questions? Students said yes to this and related participation questions in 14 of the samples. One study did find that students participated less when most of them answered the clicker questions correctly.

Student responses in a number of studies confirmed the instantaneous feedback benefit for increased understanding, and in the studies that asked whether students thought using this technology was easy, all found that students reported no trouble using clickers.

This review documents that in a range of disciplines, positive experiences with clicker technologies are being reported. That finding should motivate serious consideration of this flexible and still evolving instructional technology. This review includes references to a considerable number of studies; beyond their empirical value, they are a treasure trove of ideas and information regarding how clickers are actually being used.

Reference: Keough, S. M. (2012). Clickers in the classroom: A review and a replication. *Journal of Management Education,* 36(6), 822–847.

Reprinted from *The Teaching Professor,* Feb 2013

Keys to successful group work

Designing Group Work

Reason to read: Problems emerge in groups when the activities students are completing are poorly designed. Although a well-designed activity won't prevent all the problems, it can reduce the number significantly.

Certain common problems can emerge when students work together in groups. Here, we discuss how the group activities that are engaging students can include design features that make those problems less likely to occur or enable the group to deal with the problem.

The divide-and-conquer problem. Students who are not very committed to group work love it when they get an assignment that can be divided into equal parts, with each member responsible for one of the parts. This way, they don't have to meet or function as a group. Everybody just does their own thing and each "thing" is put in the group's folder or said during that member's four-minute part of the presentation. Group projects can be designed to prevent this problem. For example, each student in the group can be assigned a different content chunk, such as a reading, and the group must do a paper or presentation that requires integration of all the different readings.

The send-everything-to-me-and-I'll-put-it-together-for-the-group problem. The member who most often volunteers to do this for the group is the person who doesn't trust others to deliver quality work. This gives the member the chance to redo others' contributions to his or her specifications. It may solve problems, but it significantly erodes group cohesion and encourages freeloading. Group work can be designed so that everybody in the group must review and/or "sign off" on the final product.

The free-rider problem. Probably the problem that most worries faculty is when individual students let the rest of the group carry the workload. A group design that includes some sort of peer assessment or requests a clear delineation of who did what goes a long way to prevent this problem.

The don't-deliver-when-it's-due problem. This is really just another version of the free-rider problem: a member who doesn't come through with the goods when the group needs them. The design solution here is to make work due in installments so the group discovers early who doesn't deliver and can exert some peer pressure.

The we're-not-getting-along problem. This may be a problem with too many leaders and not enough followers, or a case of baggage from bad group experiences in the past. Well-designed group work empowers students to handle their own problems rather than taking everything to the teacher for adjudication. Solutions might be something as simple as a handout describing the characteristics of groups that function productively, a discussion of the interplay between individual and group responsibility, or an opportunity for representatives from individual groups to share difficulties and brainstorm solutions.

Well-designed group work does make a difference; it's just that designing good group work is a more intellectually demanding task than most teachers realize.

Reprinted from The Teaching Professor blog, Mar 24, 2009

Improving Group Projects

Reason to read: You probably shouldn't have students working in groups unless you're willing to devote some time to teaching them how to function constructively and productively in those groups. Here's a rundown of things you can do that will improve the products students produce in groups and the processes they use to do so.

Many faculty now have students do some graded work in groups. The task may be the preparation of a paper or report, the collection and analysis of data, a presentation supported with visuals, or the creation of a website, among many examples. Faculty make these assignments with high expectations. They want the groups to produce quality work—better than what students could do individually—and they want students to learn how to work productively with others. Sometimes those expectations are realized, but most of the time, there is room for improvement—sometimes lots of it. To that end, here's a set of suggestions for improving group projects. A list in the article referenced below provided a starting place for these recommendations.

Emphasize the importance of teamwork. Before the groups are formed and the task is set out, teachers should make clear why this particular assignment is being done in groups. Students are still regularly reporting in survey data that they believe teachers use groups so they don't have to teach or have as much work to grade. In contrast, most of us are using groups because employers in many fields want employees who can work with others—others they don't know, others they may not like, others with different views, and others with different skills and capabilities.

Teach teamwork skills. Most students don't come to group work knowing how to function effectively in groups. Whether in handouts, online resources, or discussions in class, teachers need to talk about the responsibilities members have to the group (how sometimes, individual goals and priorities must be relinquished in favor of group goals) and about what members have the right to expect from their groups. Students need strategies for dealing with members who are not doing their fair share. They need ideas on constructively resolving disagreement. They need advice on time management.

Use team-building exercises to build cohesive groups. Members need the chance to get to know each other and they should be encouraged to talk about how they'd like to work together. Sometimes a discussion of worst group experiences makes clear to everyone that there are behaviors to avoid. This might be followed with a discussion of what each individual member needs from the group in order to do their best work. Things like picking a group name and creating a logo also help create a sense of identity for the group, which in turn fosters the commitment groups need from their members in order to succeed.

Thoughtfully consider group formation. Most students prefer forming their own groups, and in some studies, these groups have been shown to be more productive. In other research, students in these groups "enjoy" the experience of working together, but they don't always get a lot done. In most professional contexts, people don't get to choose their project partners. If the goal is for students to learn how to work with others they don't know, then the teacher should form the groups. There are many ways groups can be formed and many criteria that can be used to assemble them. Groups should be formed in a way that furthers the learning goals of the group activity.

Make the workload reasonable and the goals clear. Yes, the task can be larger than what one individual can complete. But students without a lot of group work experience struggle with large, complex tasks. Whatever the task, the teacher's goals and objectives should be clear. Students shouldn't have to spend a lot of time trying to figure out what they are supposed to be doing.

Consider roles for group members. Not all the literature recommends assigning roles, although some does. Roles can emerge on their own as members see what functions the group needs and step up to fill those roles. However, this doesn't always happen when students are new to group work. The teacher can decide on the necessary roles and suggest them, with the group ultimately deciding who does what. The teacher can assign the roles, but should realize that assigning roles doesn't guarantee that students will assume those roles. Assigned roles can stay the same or can rotate. However, once they're implemented, roles are taken more seriously if groups are required to report who filled what role in the group.

Provide some class time for meetings. It is very hard for students to orchestrate their schedules. Part of what they need to be taught about group work is the importance of coming to meetings with an agenda (some expectation about what needs to get done). They also need to know that significant amounts of work can be done in short periods of time, provided the group knows what needs to be done next. Working online is also an option, but being able to convene even briefly in class gives groups the chance to touch base and get organized for the next steps.

Request interim reports and group process feedback. One of the group's first tasks ought to be the creation of a timeline—what they expect to have done by when. That timeline should guide instructor requests for progress reports from the group and the reports should be supported with evidence. It's not good enough for the group to say it is collecting references; a list of references should be submitted with the report. Students should report individually on how well the group is working together, including their contributions to the group. What else could they contribute that would make the group function even more effectively?

Require individual members to keep track of their contributions. The final project should include a report from every individual member identifying their contribution to the project. If two members report contributing the same thing, the teacher defers to the student who has evidence to support what the student claims to have done.

Include peer assessment in the evaluation process. What a student claims to have contributed to the group and its final product can also be verified via a peer assessment in which members rate and/or rank the contributions of others. A formative peer assessment early in the process can help members redress what the group might identify as problems they are experiencing early on.

Students (like the rest of us) aren't born knowing how to work well in a group. Fortunately, it's a skill that can be taught and learned. Teacher design and management of group work on projects can do much to ensure that the lessons students learn about working with others are the ones that will serve them well next time they work in groups.

Reference: Hansen, R. S. (2006). Benefits and problems with student teams: Suggestions for improve team projects. *Journal of Education for Business,* September/October, 11–19.

Reprinted from *The Teaching Professor,* Jun/Jul 2013

Peer Assessment in Small Groups

Reason to read: Peer assessment takes care of lots of problems in student groups—students riding on the work others do in the group, for example. Students don't like peer assessment—they aren't used to critiquing their peers, but it's a skill worth developing. The best place to start is with feedback on specific concrete actions that contribute to group productivity.

Need a good list of behaviors that students can assess when they work with each other in small groups? Diane Baker, in an excellent article on peer assessment in small groups, reviewed a wide collection of instruments and found that although the number of items varied, most included some iteration of these eight behavioral components.

- Attended group meetings, as in were available to meet, came on time, and did not leave early
- Were dependable, as in met deadlines, did what they said they would do
- Delivered, as in did the work they were assigned and did it well
- Made an effort or made an extra effort, as in volunteered for work, actively engaged in helping the group get the work done, took up the slack when need be
- Worked cooperatively with others, as in communicated well with group members, got along with everybody, shared information, and listened
- Helped the group manage conflict, as in worked to resolve interpersonal or group conflict, helped to create a constructive environment where conflict was managed to the benefit of the group
- Contributed, as in brought knowledge, experience, and/or skills that helped the group accomplish its task

- Helped the group achieve its goals, as in helped with identification of goals, then monitored progress and finally assessed achievement

If students don't have a lot of experience assessing each other's performance, then using instruments that identify concrete, observable behaviors is probably a good place to start. Not only does this develop students' observation skills, it is a more descriptive and less judgmental approach to evaluation: either the group member showed up to meetings or not.

Reference: Baker, D. L., (2008). Peer assessment in small groups: A comparison of methods. Journal of Management Education, 32(2), 183–209.

Reprinted from The Teaching Professor blog, Sept 5, 2008

CHAPTER 4

•

Creating Climates for Learning

Introduction

What's a climate for learning and how do you create it? The climate metaphor is a vexing one. It's useful in that it makes clear that learning is strongly influenced by the conditions in which it occurs. It's like what the weather does to behavior: If it's cold, we get a sweater. If it's hot, we take the sweater off. We don't think about what we're doing; what's happening in the environment makes the necessary action obvious. If you get a new GPS and you want to use it, you need to learn how. You don't need a required assignment. You don't need an externally imposed deadline. You don't need bonus points. All that stuff doesn't matter when you have a need to know, and that's what the climate metaphor clarifies for us. We need classrooms where the "climate" makes the need to know obvious and compelling.

What the metaphor doesn't do so well is specify what exactly it is we are talking about when we refer to classroom climate, environment, or atmosphere. If we aren't talking about the actual weather, then what are we referring to? And that's the question a lot of these resources attempt to answer.

There are two intriguing factors about classroom climate. First, it's not created by announcement. You can say you'd like to have one in the course, but saying doesn't make it so. It created by what you do—a case of actions speaking louder than words. Secondly, teachers can show leadership when it comes to creating climates for learning, but teachers cannot create the climate without students participating in the process. You can say you want lots of participation, but if nobody speaks, you don't have it. I told my students something a teacher once said to me: "This isn't my class. It isn't your class. This is our class, and together we'll decide what happens here."

Although we're in it together with students, the teacher's presence plays a powerful role—one you don't want to underestimate. Students relate to teachers as persons, and **being present in the classroom, online, and during office hours** involves more than your physical presence. People can be present but not really there, and this is a particular hazard with teaching.

You can get to know the material so well and fit into your teaching role so comfortably that even though you're there, you're not. You're going through the motions, doing what you've done oh so many times before. You're hearing students but not really listening—you know what they're going to ask and you know how you're going to answer. Unfortunately, it is easy to tell when people are doing what they've done countless times before: think about flight attendants and the safety briefing, think about guides on a tour bus. Students don't necessarily need our presence; they need us to be present. They us to be with them as they explore this new and difficult content for the first time. They want us to put aside what we're doing and attend to them when they come to the office. They want us to answer their e-mails. They don't want us to act as if they're just another of the countless students we've encountered. Most of us want to be there for students, but we get tired; we're overworked, and being there takes focus and energy. But we need to be there because when we are, learning is a more likely outcome

It's easy to get fixated on **classroom management** issues. Students can be disruptive and disrespectful. They can come to class late and leave early. They can fall asleep, have lunch, or do homework for other classes. They can talk, text, and keep their attention focused on their devices. The typical faculty response to all of this is a set of policies, laid out in detail on the syllabus. Students are told what they should do and what they can't do in no uncertain terms. Most students follow the policies, but there are those who don't, and that means the policies must be enforced.

A few things to remember: This is another case where your actions are way more convincing than your words. So if you don't accept late homework and it says that on the syllabus, then don't accept it, especially at the front of the room with the whole class present. And second, policies are pretty hard to enforce. Yes, you can impose penalties—points off for late papers, marked absent if you come in late—but if the penalty doesn't bother the student, it's probably not going to change the behavior. And when push comes to shove, short of a physical alteration, you really cannot prevent a student from leaving class early. It's a good idea to be clear in your thinking about what you can and cannot make a student do. Power struggles with students end up having very little to do with learning.

What is a learning climate and how do you create it?

Classroom Climates

by Maryellen Weimer

Reason to read: If it's not climate in the weather sense, then what is it?

I did a workshop this week on climates for learning. It's a session I love doing. Nobody argues with the need to have one in the classroom and everywhere else around campus. But most of us haven't gotten past the metaphor (we aren't talking about the "weather" in our classroom, even though we do regularly refer to the "atmosphere" in class and the "environment" on campus). When we refer to the climate for learning, what are we talking about?

In most sessions, faculty struggle with a definition, few offering anything beyond one-word descriptors that identify characteristics of learning climates. "Safe," someone volunteers: "students feel safe in the classroom." "Respect," somebody else says. "A warm place," which I gently point out is more of the weather metaphor.

The definition I use for the climate for learning comes out of the research of Barry Fraser, who did extensive work on classroom climate during the 1980s. Fraser defines classroom climate as a series of psycho-social relationships that exist between faculty and students collectively and individually. Below you'll find a reference to the instrument Fraser and colleagues developed to measure climate in the classroom. The instrument gives form and substance to the elusive and abstract idea of classroom climate. It contains seven sub-scales that identify those actions teachers and students take that promote the climate for learning in the classroom. Here are three examples: "personalization," what Fraser calls the interactions between the teacher and students and how it is the teacher expresses concern and care for students; "involvement," which assesses the extent to which students participate in the activities of the classroom; and "student cohesiveness," meaning how well students know and are connected with each other.

After the session, someone asked if there was any recent research on classroom climate. I know of another instrument published in 1994 but not much else. I gently challenged this faculty member to take a look at Fraser's instrument. I don't see anything in it that is no longer relevant or that isn't part of what makes a climate for learning in classrooms today. Good research stands the test of time, and I think this work is a great example.

One of the things I really like about the Fraser instrument is that it asks students to identify the classroom climate in a class and then rate the same characteristics in terms of their perceptions of the preferred climate. I've used this instrument for years, and I think teachers benefit most from the feedback it offers if they complete the instrument along with students. It's good to discover how your take on the climate in a particular classroom compares with what students report they're experiencing.

Reference: Fraser, B. J., Treagust, D. F., & Dennis, N. C. (1986). Development of an instrument for assessing classroom psychosocial environment at universities and colleges. *Studies in Higher Education*, 11(1), 43–53.

Reprinted from The Teaching Professor blog, June 17, 2010

Factors that Lead to Rapport

by Maryellen Weimer

Reason to read: If actions are what create classroom climate, then what actions do teachers and students need to take? Consider these options related to establishing rapport, which is an essential part of climates that promote learning.

"Rapport" is one of those words faculty frequently toss out when I ask them to describe the climate for learning in a classroom. I do agree (and so does the research) that rapport is something that benefits efforts to learn. It motivates students to expend more effort while at the same time keeping them engaged and involved. But what is rapport? Understanding the term makes developing it more likely. To that end, consider this list of factors leading to good rapport generated from online interviews with 40 faculty (mostly in business fields). These are examples from a longer list, but they are listed in order of importance.

Respect – Faculty and students show respect for each other.

Caring – Faculty care about learning. They want their students to be successful. Faculty see students as individuals, each with unique personal circumstances.

Approachability – Faculty must show (not just tell) students that they are interested in working with them.

Open communication – Faculty must be honest and open about their policies and instructional practices.

Mutual openness – Faculty share information about themselves and seek out information about individual students—from their aspirations to where they call home.

Interest in student success – Faculty monitor student progress and intervene with offers of help when students are floundering.

Trust – Students learn that they can trust faculty. If faculty announce that papers will be back next Wednesday, they are returned next Wednesday.

Keeping it real – Faculty act like the humans they are. If they are mistaken, they make that admission.

Patience – Faculty willingly answer questions they have already answered. They know that it takes students time to "get it" and that learning can be a stressful endeavor.

Reference: Granitz, N. A., Koernig, S. K., & Harich, K. R. (2009). Now it's personal: Antecedents and outcomes of rapport between business faculty and their students. *Journal of Marketing Education,* 31(1), 52¬–65.

Reprinted from The Teaching Professor blog, April 9, 2009

Being present in class, online, and during office hours

Witness the Struggle: The Gifts of Presence, Silence, and Choice

by Patricia Kohler-Evans and Candice Barnes, University of Central Arkansas

Reason to read: Here's an eloquent description of what it means to be present. The good news? The actions involved are simple and straightforward.

I have long pondered a phrase I learned from a mentor: "Witness the struggle." Frances, my mentor, used the phrase when she talked about working with students in emotional pain. She referred to those students who sometimes lash out in frustration over missed assignments, family dynamics, or other stressful life issues. As a career educator, I have a deep desire to help students and a strong tendency to offer solutions and make suggestions. I want to fix their problems and tell them what to do. The wise words of this phrase offer a more powerful and profound answer to the part of me that thinks I need to rescue students. Its simple urging suggests that I be fully engaged and present, that I use silence to clear a space, and that I guard against telling students what to do. More often than not, students simply need to know that their voice counts, that they have been heard, and that who they are matters.

Be fully engaged and present. How often do we look up during office hours to see a troubled-looking student standing at the door? He needs help, but we are working against the clock to prepare the next lecture, or reviewing materials to be discussed in an upcoming committee meeting. As

I write, I'm seeing numerous student faces: some looking hurt, others angry, some seeming as though they just might implode. Our students experience strong emotions. These faces remind me that at times, I have been abrupt, and at other times, I have been inviting.

Being fully engaged and present suggests that I stop what I am doing and give students my full attention. Glancing up from the computer while continuing to type or looking at the clock does not suggest that I am present. Being fully present means just that. For the next 5 or 30 minutes, I have nothing more pressing than the time I give to my student. Certainly, I may state that I have 10 minutes before my next appointment, but for those 10 minutes, my student's voice is the only one sending messages to my brain. I sit with him, and I keep my thoughts on what he is saying. We may schedule another time for a deeper discussion, but the time I spend with him belongs to him alone.

Use silence to clear space. Let's face it, we are teachers, and we like to talk. That's how we make our living. We walk into our classes and begin by opening our mouths. Our students benefit greatly from the knowledge we impart; it helps prepare them for their careers. However, as important as our wisdom is, when students come to us with their misunderstandings; problems with assignment deadlines; or difficulties balancing family, work, and school, what they need from us, in addition to our presence, is our silence. I am not referring to the crossed-arm, closed body postures that convey contempt and disdain. This silence is a quiet indicating that as teacher or advisor, I want to understand and will listen without interruption or assumption. I want my student to be heard without my butting in. The gift of silence is offered, and an invitation given for the student's voice to enter into the space created. By being quiet, I also become a thinking partner with my student as she begins to communicate her pressing concerns.

Refrain from giving advice. Being fully present and using silence to create space are both challenging; however, perhaps the most difficult behavior for teachers is allowing students to construct and choose their own solutions. We admonish our students to study, to read, to prepare, to work hard, to think critically to be creative, and more. We are, after all, recognized experts. We know what it takes to learn and to succeed in life. As difficult as it may seem, we must let go of this proclivity to tell our students what they need to do. Most of the time, they probably know what they should do, but they need to be heard, not to hear us. When we engage with our presence and our silence, we can ask questions that invite students to think about the choices they make and the attention they pay to competing demands. By refraining from giving advice, we are suggesting that our students are fully capable of reaching conclusions that will lead them to their desired outcomes. And we know the advice they give themselves is probably more persuasive than the advice we offer.

When we make ourselves fully present and attentive, use silence to create space, and encourage students to construct their own solutions, we are giving a gift that costs nothing, but has great value. It is the gift that lets students know how much we care.

Reprinted from *The Teaching Professor*, Apr 2012

Something to think about...
"Imagine someone at the very beginning of his or her teaching career, coming to a class session so nervous, so insecure, clinging so desperately to the teaching plan that he or she was up late working on the night before that a sort of glass wall descends and the teacher and the students remain as remote from each other as though they were in separate mediums. When we're absent, when we're not there, this, in effect, excludes students..." (p. 216).

Reference: Farber, J., (2008). Teaching and presence. Pedagogy, 8(2), 215–225.

Who and what needs to be managed?

Why Policies Fail to Promote Better Learning Decisions

by Lolita Paff, Penn State, Berks

Reason to read: Faculty tend to spend a lot of time considering what policies they'll need for the course to run smoothly. Often they err on the side of too many rather than not enough. Before making policy decisions, it's wise to consider how policies can actually get in the way of learning.

Policies are necessary. They serve as a warning to students: this is what will happen if you are absent, miss an exam, turn work in late, text or surf the Web during class, and the like. Most institutions recommend teachers spell out consequences in their syllabi. Some schools employ institution-wide policies for certain behaviors like academic dishonesty. If policies are supposed to prevent these unproductive behaviors, why do students still engage in them? Are there reasons why policies don't work?

Policies don't teach students why these behaviors hurt their effort to learn. Despite extensive evidence to the contrary, many students believe their learning is unaffected by technology distractions. "No screens" policies are aimed, at least in part, at minimizing distractions that hurt students' learning (their own and peers'). But policies aren't nearly as powerful as an activity that demonstrates the effects of distraction.

Split the class into two groups. One is allowed to text; the other turns their phones off. After the lecture, students complete a short quiz. Ellis, Daniels, and Jauregui (2010) report that students in the phones-off group score significantly higher. Differences in points or cores will grab tudents' attention and are more likely to get them thinking about their mobile technology use in and out of class than a "no screens" policy.

Policies tend to be reactive, not proactive. A student engages in a behavior that isn't addressed in the syllabus. A common reaction is to add a new policy or rewrite the existing one for the following term. The syllabus grows by a few lines. But the new policy assumes future students will behave in the same way. Different students may behave in different ways that are, again, not covered in the policy. And the student whose negative learning behavior precipitated the new policy may not be in future courses. Has the new policy accomplished anything for that student?

Sometimes these behaviors are one-offs. No policy fix is necessary. Generally, a "new" negative learning behavior would be more effectively addressed if the teacher talked with the student individually or thought about what might have caused the behavior, then identified strategies to prevent it. Adding or editing policies is a quick fix, but not one that advances student learning.

Policies that attempt to cover every possible scenario encourage loophole finding. Think IRS tax code. Here, the focus is on grades, lost points, and consequences, instead of on learning and the learner. Highly punitive policies may encourage fraudulent excuse-making. Meanwhile, inflexible policies often have an implied message that's probably unintentional: "I don't care what is going on in your life. This is the rule. Deal with it." To develop students as independent and mature learners, teachers need to go beyond policies to employ strategies and practices that allow students to learn from their behaviors, not just suffer the consequences.

Learning is personal. Harsh language and rigid rules diminish community and send a message of distrust, and generally suggest teachers don't believe students will do work without the threat of penalties. Worse, these policies suggest faculty don't believe the best about students. This leads to students believing teachers don't like or care for them.

A focus on rules and policies shifts interest away from learning. One way to redirect attention is to share the learning and professional rationales that underpin deadlines and policies. Provide opportunities for students to have input about some assignment details or a few due dates. A policy students help to shape is one they own, and one they are more likely to live up to.

Policies are unsupportive of students' efforts to become self-directed learners. Policies, especially those with harsh consequences, may reduce the number of times students arrive to class late or show up unprepared. But what happens when the policy stick (or carrot, for that matter) is removed? If students are only behaving in a certain way because of a penalty or reward, what have they learned about the value of the behavior (like reading) as part of learning?

Fortunately, there are teacher practices that help students mature as learners while promoting positive learning behaviors. Teachers can incorporate homework logs, assign learning reflections, facilitate student goal setting and project planning, and employ contract grading. Each of these strategies increases student ownership of learning and advances their development as independent learners.

Consider how a strict policy commands attendance. Instead of, or in addition to, policy, provide data that shows the negative correlation between the number of absences and exam scores. Or provide the dates on which specific topics and concepts were covered and tell students the dates they were absent. If students see that they lost points on topics that were learned during their absence, they can see the consequences of skipping class. This kind of evidence teaches more about the value of attending class than does a policy requiring it.

Supplement course deadlines with a conversation about learning behaviors like procrastination and time management. Share your own strategies for juggling multiple responsibilities and meeting short- and long-term commitments. Could students share their successful and not-so-successful time management experiences? Have students been asked what would help them get the work done in a timely way? Discussions about punctuality, procrastination, and time management advance students' understanding of how they work and learn.

Policies are necessary. It's important for students to understand what is expected of them and the consequences when they fall short. But to develop students as independent and mature learners, teachers need to go beyond policies to employ strategies and practices that allow students to learn from their behaviors, not just suffer the consequences.

Reference: Ellis, Y., Daniels, B., & Jauregui, A., 2010. The effect of multitasking on grade performance of business students. *Research in Higher Education Journal,* 8, 1–10.

Reprinted from Faculty Focus, September 28, 2015

CHAPTER 5

•

Teaching Online

Introduction

Never done it before? If you've never taught online before, remember this: everybody else was once in your shoes. Given the amount of online teaching happening now, there's lots of experience to learn from, and the resources here provide some examples. Course design is an important part of success in all courses, but it's crucial when the course is online. You aren't always there to provide direction, so what students need to do and when should be spelled out clearly. Teaching is definitely different when the teacher and students are only known to each other electronically. As you can imagine, effective written communication gains a whole new level of importance.

Teaching online has its challenges, starting with the need to develop a sense of community, to make it truly feel like a class. The teacher provides leadership, connecting with students and getting them connected to each other. Participation in online courses mostly occurs via online discussion, which needs to be understood for what it shares with face-to-face discussion and what makes it unique. Online exchanges can lack spontaneity and often move forward according to a teacher-provided script: teacher provides a prompt, students respond once to the teacher and once to another student's response—this can become **the posting-of-comments-but-not-having-a-discussion** problem. But online discussion also has its advantages. It's an easier venue for reticent students, and written responses tend to be prepared more carefully than verbal ones, which can ratchet up the caliber of the exchanges.

Online courses offer educational opportunities to many students who are unable to go college in the traditional way. They offer teachers the convenience of teaching from home and the chance to present content to students in an entirely different way. With a better understanding about what online courses are and aren't, we can make these classes an effective and engaging option for teachers and learners alike.

Never taught online before?

Top 10 Rules for Developing Your First Online Course

by John Orlando

Reason to read: Here's great advice for beginners from an experienced online teacher.

Years of helping faculty pass to the dark side of online education have taught me a few simple rules that I browbeat (in a collegial way) into all new online teachers.

Rule 1: Provide Extra Detail in Your Online Syllabus

Most of us spend much of the first day of class going through the syllabus, taking time to elaborate on different points, and answering questions as we go along. Online classrooms lack this time, and so the syllabus must be more detailed than it would be for a face-to-face class, especially when it comes to procedures. You can also preempt problems and save time answering questions by creating a discussion forum devoted to common questions about the class itself.

Rule 2: Begin with Community Building

Despite appearances, online education is (should be) a fundamentally communal endeavor, with discussion taking center stage. But discussion requires trust, which can be built through community-building exercises. Some educators even recommend spending the first two weeks on community building, asserting that it will pay for itself in better performance over the remainder of the course.

Rule 3: Design for the Web

I remember building my first online course by transcribing the lectures from my face-to-face course into text. Somehow the students managed to get through them, bless their hearts. But of course, the online environment is fundamentally visual, built on videos, interaction, exploration, etc. All effective communication requires an understanding of the rules of that environment. Don't view the online environment through the paradigm of the face-to-face environment. Rather, design for the web.

Rule 4: Account for Different Systems

It's easy to forget that webpages operate differently on different browsers, and especially on different devices. Ask your instructional designers to go over your course to confirm that everything will work on different systems. It's a good idea to check in with them before designing content so that they can give you a template that will work.

Rule 5: If Someone Can Say it Better than You, Then Let Them

The first time I taught medical ethics, I wrote a long description of the Human Genome Project for my students to read. It took me hours and was boring. Then I discovered that the National Institutes of Health (NIH) had a beautiful website covering everything in my document and more. I could have saved myself a lot of time and provided better content by sending students to the NIH website.

Faculty often think they must develop every piece of content from scratch, but nearly all of the information in their heads is available somewhere else. Use the Internet to your advantage by curating, rather than creating, content whenever possible.

Rule 6: Use a Consistent Format

Humans are fundamentally pattern-recognition animals, meaning that we will look for patterns to help guide our actions. Create a template of what you will want from students in each module and follow it. It might be that your modules start with a video overview of the material, links to various content, three discussion questions, etc. Changes in midstream invariably lead to students missing content or assignments.

Rule 7: Remember the Workload Parameters

Some faculty seem to think that they need to "make up" for the online format by assigning extra work, or maybe the cornucopia of material available on the Web makes them want to assign all of it, lest a student miss some detail that they may need 20 years down the line. Either way, faculty commonly assign too much content in an online class. If you assign too much, students will only view part of it, and the part they choose as more important may not be what you think is most important. Define a reasonable workload range and stay within it.

Rule 8: Provide Content in Different Formats Whenever Possible

Although the premise that people have different learning styles is somewhat controversial, I've found that different people prefer different types of content. For this reason, as well as for ADA purposes, it's a good idea to present content in different formats whenever possible. This could be as simple as providing a transcript to accompany a video.

Rule 9: Mix Content and Activities

One disadvantage of the traditional college lecture is that it separates content from engagement: the teacher talks for 50 minutes or longer, and the students engage with the material later as homework. But this is not how we learn. We need practice and reflection every 20 minutes or so to move knowledge from our short-term memory to our long-term memory. In the online classroom, systems like VoiceThread or Articulate Storyline are ideal for allowing teachers to intersperse activities with their content to enable immediate application and better retention.

Rule of Rules (10): It Takes Longer than You Think

All faculty members, including me, underestimate how long it will take them to develop online content. I tell faculty to develop their content during the semester prior to the course going live, and earlier if at all possible.

Reprinted from Faculty Focus, March 3, 2013

Five Factors that Affect Online Student Motivation

by Rob Kelly

Reason to read: Motivation is an issue in all courses and those conducted online are no exception. Here's a good description of ways motivation can be increased when students are dealing with the content electronically.

Understanding what motivates online learners is important because motivated students are more likely to engage in activities that help them learn and achieve, says Brett Jones, associate professor of educational psychology at Virginia Tech. Based on an extensive review of the literature on student motivation, Jones has developed the MUSIC model of student motivation, which identifies five main factors that contribute to student motivation: eMpowerment, Usefulness, Success, Interest, and Caring.

"The primary purpose of the model is to provide instructors with a guide that they can use to make intentional decisions about the design of their courses," Jones says. In an interview with Online Classroom, Jones explained his model and its implications for online course design. We're providing an excerpt of it here.

1. eMpowerment. Students feel empowered when they feel that they have some control over some aspects of their learning. This can involve giving students choices. "Is there some way that we can give students at least a little bit of control by giving them choices? Is there a way to give students some option to bring in something from their own lives or make some decision about a topic within that narrow assignment that lets them feel like they have some control over it?" Jones asks.

Jones cites an example from an online personal health course: The instructor has students either take an online assessment or attend one or two workshops on campus related to the course's learning objectives. This allows students the opportunity to choose their activities while still staying within the framework and goals of the course.

2. Usefulness. Students need to see that the course is useful and relevant to them within the course and beyond. In some cases, it will be obvious that the skills students acquire through a course will directly contribute to their success in a chosen career field. In other cases, that connection will not be as clear. Jones recommends being explicit about how the skills and knowledge students acquire in the course can be applied beyond school. One way to do this is to have students interview professionals in their chosen careers about what skills and knowledge contributed to their success.

3. Success. Students need to feel that they can succeed in the course if they make a reasonable effort. The instructor can help students succeed by setting expectations, providing feedback, and facilitating the course so that students have access to additional resources if needed. "What resources do you have available for them to succeed? If you think ahead, you can know what problems students typically run into. A lot of times, you can create additional documents or videos that explain the more difficult concepts," Jones says.

4. Interest. There are two types of interest that contribute to student motivation: situational interest and individual interest. Situational interest refers to an aspect of a course that is enjoyable or fun. For example, Jones incorporates articles from Psychology Today related to the course's learning objectives to vary the tone and provide a different perspective from the textbook. "These are just little side readings that don't take a lot of time and that might help students see how the [concept] might apply to the real world," he notes.

Situational interest can be enhanced by novelty and emotions. "We as humans are attracted to things that are novel. If you have something that can engender emotion so you get people fired up about a topic or issue that relates to your learning objectives, that can really draw people in. We want to trigger their interest so that they pay attention enough and are interested enough while they are engaged in it," Jones says.

Situational interest is often short-lived, but it can lead to longer-term individual interest, which refers to how the content relates to the individual. For example, a student taking a course within his or her major might have a strong individual interest in the content based on how the content relates to who they are and what they aspire to. A mechanical engineering major may have a strong individual interest in a mechanical engineering course because she sees herself as a mechanical engineer and thinks, "I'm interested in it because it's who I am."

Meanwhile, it is possible for a student to have an individual interest in a course but not a situational interest. A student might think, for example, "I want to be a mechanical engineer, but this is boring."

Remember that interest isn't universal. "We assume that students think a particular subject is fascinating or that everybody's curious about it, but that's not the case," Jones says.

5. Caring. Students need to feel that the instructor (and other students) care that they learn. Jones assumed that although caring is a big motivator for children, it would not play a large role caring was the number one predictor of online instructor ratings. Instead, he says, "It turns out that caring is very important even for adult learners."

Jones recommends providing regular feedback and asking students whether they feel that they're getting the support they need.

Reprinted from Faculty Focus, August 10, 2012

Tips for Building Social Presence in Your Online Class

by Oliver Dreon, Millersville University, Pa.

Reason to read: How can you create the sense of a teacher being present and students being in a course with other students when the connections are only electronic? It seems like a big challenge, but in reality, there's lots of ways to create this sense of community.

You've been assigned your first online class to teach and you feel like you're ready. You've done your homework and learned the ins and outs of the institution's course management system. You've structured your content in purposeful ways and developed thoughtful guiding questions to situate student learning and motivate students. When the class starts, however, you realize that while everything is technically functioning correctly, many of the students are not engaged. While you were looking forward to teaching online and interacting with students, the students are approaching your course as if it's an independent study. This wasn't what you anticipated when you agreed to teach online!

In their framework outlining educational experiences for students, Garrison, Anderson, and Archer (2000) identify and explain the critical elements of a Community of Inquiry that supports instruction and learning. The elements include: cognitive presence, social presence, and teaching presence. For online classes, many instructors new to the online world tend to focus on cognitive presence and teaching presence, overlooking the necessity of the social presence. They'll build great online modules that help students enhance their understanding of course content but forget to attend to the critical social aspects that engage students and foster community building. While these aspects can happen naturally in face-to-face courses, they must be intentionally built into online classes.

Here are five ways you can build social presence in your online class:

1. **Have your online students introduce themselves.** This may sound simple, but the first module of my online courses asks students to introduce themselves to their peers. I create a discussion board where students share short introductions with the group, either through text or through a short multimedia production using Fotobabble, MyBrainShark, or some other Web 2.0 tool. I usually try to connect the introductions to course content in some informal way to assess students' prior knowledge and experience with the material. More than anything, these introductions are designed to foster open communication amongst students outside of course content.

2. **Introduce yourself to your students.** When I ask my students to create short introductions of themselves, I offer my own introduction as an example. I also create a short orientation video where I provide an overview of the course and share a little about myself. Presented as a short video in which students hear my voice, this introduction allows students to connect with me outside of the written text that I provide for most of the class material.

3. **Create a "common area" for off-topic discussions.** In a face-to-face class, it's easy to engage in off-topic discussions. Students walking into the classroom will argue about last night's football game, discuss the latest movies, or talk about their favorite music. This type of engagement is extracurricular, but it can help students build relationships that are advantageous inside the classroom. Without purposeful inclusion of risk-free environments for sharing, online students' affective needs will not be met and they may not fully engage with course content or with their classmates. In my online classes, I create a discussion board labeled "Common Area" or "Water Cooler" and offer some guidance on the purpose of the area. While I'll often peek in to add a question or respond to a post, I generally give the students some free rein over this forum.

4. **Use synchronous tools for office hours.** Most course management systems offer chat rooms or synchronous online classrooms as tools for teaching and communication. I schedule online office hours during which students can meet with me to discuss course content and ask questions. While not every student takes advantage of the office hours, publishing their availability communicates to students that I am committed to their success in the course.

5. Don't be the center of every discussion. Many new online instructors try to respond to every post in a discussion board. This habit can actually limit student-to-student interaction and discussion. In a face-to-face class, few instructors would break up lively classroom discussions by evaluating every remark from students. In online classes, however, instructors will do exactly that. Instead of excessively participating in discussion boards, provide some thought-provoking questions and allow the students to discuss course content openly on their own. Offer guidance when necessary and communicate that you're present in the discussion through carefully chosen posts. Give the students some space to interact with one another and build their understanding through collaborating with their classmates.

References: Garrison, D. R., Anderson, T., & Archer, W. (2000). Critical inquiry in a text-based environment: Computer conferencing in higher education. The Internet and Higher Education, 2(2-3), 87–105.

Reprinted from Faculty Focus, May 13, 2013

Recommended Resource
Journal of Online Teaching and Learning
This open-access journal (meaning you don't need a subscription) offers a wide range of articles that cover online teaching and learning issues. There are research pieces, advice on course design, online testing and assignment options, ways of preventing cheating, accounts of faculty experiences, and references to lots of other resources. For faculty new and not so new to teaching online, it's an invaluable resource.

Discussion that's more than posting comments

Art and Science of Successful Online Discussions

by Stephanie Maher Palenque and Meredith DeCosta, Grand Canyon University

> *Reason to read: Online discussions share features with classroom discussions, but they aren't the same. They need to be thought of and designed differently. Otherwise, you will likely have students posting comments but not having animated, interesting, and informative discussions.*

Faculty use asynchronous discussions to extend and enhance instructional practices in the online classroom. It is widely reported that online discussions play an integral role in facilitating students' learning, as well as fostering dialogue, critical thinking, and reflective inquiry (Kayler & Weller, 2007; Morris, Finnegan, & Sz-Shyan, 2005). Despite faculty's knowledge that discussion forums can serve as a useful learning tool, online discussions are not easy to establish and manage.

The Science of Online Discussions

Our working knowledge regarding distance education suggests that productive discussions are essential to learning in an asynchronous online environment. Online discussions effectively take the place of face-to-face classroom discussion. It has even been suggested that, if well facilitated, online discussions may allow for more in-depth and thoughtful learning than is possible in a face-to-face setting (Hawkes, 2006). Gao, Wang, and Sun

(2009) contend that in a productive online discussion, it is essential for participants to embrace the following four dispositions:

1. **Discuss to comprehend.** Cognitive efforts such as questioning, interpreting, elaborating, or relating information to prior knowledge should be the focus in any productive discussion. According to cognitive psychologists, students are more likely to understand and retain information when they participate in these cognitive activities (Gao, Zhang, & Franklin, 2013).
2. **Discuss to critique.** Students' conflicting perspectives should be developed and examined in any productive discussion. Knowledge acquisition originates from cognitive conflicts in social interactions. These conflicts not only occur between students but also between an individual's existing knowledge and new information encountered in discussions with other students. The real learning takes place when students re-examine their original positions on an issue and explore new resolutions. (Gao, Zhang, & Franklin, 2013).
3. **Discuss to construct knowledge.** Gao, Zhang, and Franklin (2013) suggest that a productive discussion should offer students ample opportunities for interaction and collaboration with classmates. From a social constructivist perspective, individuals do not learn in isolation. It is only through interaction that a richer understanding of the topic will develop.
4. **Discuss to share.** Productive learning takes place when students are part of a larger, active community. A community of learners, which represents the ideal discussion forum environment, is one in which students embrace a sense of belonging, support each other, develop shared values, and enjoy their shared identity (Gao, Zhang, & Franklin, 2013).

The Art of Online Discussions

Along with science comes its partner: art. People who aren't familiar with online teaching and learning will often ask, "Is it possible to mirror intellectual conversations held with students in a campus classroom in the online environment?" and "Can we engage in the subtleties of face-to-face dialogue in the online classroom?" Our answer is, "Yes." Although students in the online classroom are separated by time and space, thoughtfully formulated discussions can close this gap. The following represent strategies to transform you into an online discussion forum artist:

1. **Touch all students in the forum.** In most conversations, we acknowledge all participants, even those who are not speaking, by making eye contact, nodding, and responding as needed. The same applies to an online discussion. All students contribute in some way to the forum during a course; it is the teacher's responsibility to acknowledge their efforts. Recognition can include a congratulatory post, a note of thanks, or a question or scenario designed to further thinking.
2. **Know what each student needs.** What students say (and do not say) in the forum communicates their comfort level in the course. A student who actively participates in the forums may need the instructor to elevate his or her thinking by artfully challenging perceptions and impressions. A student who expresses confusion about the content in the forums may benefit from a Classroom Assessment Technique (Angelo & Cross, 1993) to help the instructor gauge the point of confusion and reveal gaps in the student's current knowledge.
3. **Be mindful of possibilities.** Postings are not one-size-fits-all. As online instructors, we risk hindering progress when we only award credit for posts that are lengthy, particularly at the undergraduate level. We always try not to penalize students who opt to take a brief turn in the conversation as long as the post is substantive, of merit, and adds to the discussion.
4. **Know when to lead and when to be led.** There are times when we want to guide the discussion and times when we should allow students to carry the weight. One common mistake instructors make in the online classroom is to attempt to drive every conversation. Occasionally, students may need to take charge in order to learn the material.

Science and art are natural partners—both are a means of investigating the world around us. When instructors make a concerted effort to balance both the science and art of facilitating a productive, enriching online discussion among a community of learners, the rewards are abundant.

References:

Angelo, T. A., & Cross, K. P. (1993). *Classroom assessment techniques: A handbook for college teachers.* San Francisco, CA: Jossey-Bass.

Gao, F., Zhang, T., & Franklin, T. (2013). Designing asynchronous online discussion environments: Recent progress and possible future directions. *British Journal of Educational Technology, 44*(3), 469–483.

Hawkes, M. (2006). Linguistic discourse variables as indicators of reflective online interaction. *American Journal of Distance Education,* 20(4), 231–244.

Kayler, M. & Weller, K. (2007). Pedagogy, self-assessment, and online discussion groups. *Journal of Educational Technology & Society,* 10(1), 136–147.

Morris, K.V., Finnegan, C. & Sz-Shyan, W. (2005). Tracking student behavior, persistence, and achievement in online courses. *Internet and Higher Education,* 8(3), 221–231.

Reprinted from Faculty Focus, August 11, 2014

Online Discussion Questions That Work

by John Orlando

> *Reason to read: Discussion questions are also key to successful interactions. Here are some particularly well-suited to the online environment*

Most online faculty know that discussion is one of the biggest advantages of online education. The increased think-time afforded by the asynchronous environment, coupled with the absence of public speaking fears, produces far deeper discussion than is usually found in face-to-face courses.

But many faculty undermine this natural advantage by crafting poor discussion questions. The number one mistake is to confuse a discussion question with an essay topic. What are the three criteria used to judge whether patients are competent to make a medical decision for themselves? is not a discussion question. It's an essay question and should be left to an essay assignment. I've also seen instructors turn discussion into research assignments by requiring students to cite a certain number of outside sources in order to get full credit.

I've come to believe that crafting good online discussion questions is just plain hard and that instructors rely on essay questions for lack of better ideas. Below are some question types that will help generate real discussion.

Case study

Case studies are an ideal way to illuminate the practical consequences of different concepts. For example, in a medical ethics course, I used the following:

A 72-year-old man is admitted to the hospital for a kidney transplant. His daughter is brought in as the best available match as a donor. As the man's doctor, you discover from the pre-op lab work that the daughter is not a suitable donor because she is not his biological daughter. What, if anything, do you tell the man, his wife, or the daughter?

This example provides an ideal way to explore how fundamental principles of privacy, physician honesty, and shielding a patient from harm collide in the real world. The question allows for a variety of answers, each of which takes the students deeper into the fundamental issues being taught in the course.

Controversy

Another good discussion device is to generate controversy with a statement that challenges common orthodoxy. Consider this question in an information security class:

A fundamental tenet of information security is that you must force the user to periodically change his or her password. But this practice actually undermines security. With constantly changing passwords, users are forced to write them down in an easy-to-find location or use an easy-to-guess algorithm (my street address followed by a '1,' then changed to a '2,' then changed to a '3,' etc.). We are better off letting users keep the same password indefinitely. Do you agree?

Also important is that a controversial statement needs to draw a fine line that allows for reasonable positions on both sides of the issue. It's not helpful to say something patently outrageous, such as "Passwords should not be required at all." A good statement that challenges what is being presented in the readings demonstrates that the instructor considers the students to be co-investigators and allows them to draw upon their wider knowledge base to engage the issues.

Transfer

It's been argued that the highest form of understanding is demonstrated through transfer of principles to new situations. For example, I've taught the classic "Prisoners' Dilemma" (http://pespmc1.vub.ac.be/PRISDIL.html) as part of my ethics and political theory courses. If you are not familiar with it, the upshot is that there are situations in which the rational choice for each individual involved leads to a situation that is not optimal for anyone. Think of it as the "invisible hand" in reverse.

The concept was developed as a way to understand political structures, but once you understand the concept—*really* understand it—you find that a lot of ordinary situations are prisoners' dilemmas. I'm a bike racer, and I realized that bike races are examples of the prisoners' dilemma. So a "transfer"-type discussion question might demonstrate the application of a concept to an entirely different situation by asking students to generate their own examples. Students can then evaluate how well the others' examples illustrate the concept.

Summary

A good way to end discussion threads is to post a summary of the main points, as well as your thoughts on them. Revisiting material is good for retention, and these summaries demonstrate that you are keeping abreast of the discussion. Alternatively, you can assign different students to post summaries of each discussion.

I like to do video summaries. Something about hearing a voice and seeing a face captures our attention. It requires only a cheap webcam and a few minutes of my time. Don't fret over getting it perfect—just speak your mind for a few minutes, and post it as a video.

Reprinted from Faculty Focus, November 14, 2014

Evaluating Online Discussions

Reason to read: If online discussions are not the same as in-class exchanges, then they can't be assessed using in-class criteria.

Discussion in class and online are not the same. When a comment is keyed in, more time can be involved in deciding what will be said. Online comments have more permanence. They can be read more than once and responded to more specifically. Online commentary isn't delivered orally and carries fewer of the fears associated with speaking in public. These features begin the list of what makes online discussions different. These different features also have implications for how online exchanges are assessed. What evaluation criteria are appropriate?

Two researchers offer data helpful in answering the assessment question. In their work, they decided to take a look at a collection rubrics being used to assess online discussions. They analyzed 50 rubrics they found online using various search engines and keywords. All of the rubrics in this sample were developed to assess online discussions in higher education and they did so with 153 different performance criteria. Based on a keyword analysis, the researchers grouped this collection into four major categories of criteria, each briefly discussed here.

Cognitive. Forty-four percent of the criteria were assigned to the cognitive category, which loosely represented the caliber of the intellectual thinking displayed by a student in the online exchange. Many of the criteria emphasized critical thinking, problem solving and argumentation, knowledge construction, creative thinking, and course content and readings. Many also attempted to assess the extent to which the thinking was deep, rather than superficial. Others looked at the student's ability "to apply, explain, and interpret information; to use inferences; provide conclusions; and suggest solutions." (p. 812)

Mechanical. The almost 20 percent of the criteria assigned to this category essentially assess the student's writing ability, including use of language, grammatical and spelling correctness, organization, writing style, and the use of references and citations. "Ratings that stress clarity...benefit other learners by allowing them to concentrate on the message rather than spending their time trying to decipher unclear messages." (p. 813) However, the authors worry that the emphasis on the mechanical aspects of language may detract from a student's ability to contribute in-depth analysis and reflection. They note the need for more research as to the impact of this group of assessment criteria.

Procedural/managerial. The criteria in this group focus on students' contributions and conduct in the online exchange environment. Almost 19 percent of the criteria belonged to this category. More specifically, these criteria often deal with the frequency of and timeliness of postings. Others assess the degree of respect and the extent to which students adhered to specified rules of conduct.

Interactive. About 18 percent of the criteria were placed in this category, which assesses the degree to which students are reacting to and with each other. Are students responding to what others have said, answering the questions of others, and asking others questions? Are they providing feedback? Are they using the contributions of others in their comments?

This work is not prescriptive. It does not propose which criteria are right or best. However, it does give teachers a good sense of those aspects of online interaction that are most regularly being assessed, which can be helpful in creating or revising a set of assessment criteria. Beyond what others are using, a teacher's decision should be guided by the goals and objectives of an online discussion activity. What does the teacher aspire for students to know and be able to do as a result of interacting with others in an online exchange?

References: Penny, L. & Murphy, E. (2009). Rubrics for designing and evaluating online asynchronous discussions. *British Journal of Educational Technology*, 40(5), 804–820.

Reprinted from *The Teaching Professor*, Mar 2013

CHAPTER 6

•

Quizzes, Exams, and Finals: Assessment that Promotes Learning

Introduction

Quizzes. There are good reasons for considering the use of quizzes; some of those reasons are better than others. Many faculty use quizzes to get students doing the reading regularly as opposed to all at once, and to get them coming to class on time and prepared. Quizzes accomplish those goals—not for every student, but for most. The expectation of a daily quiz motivates students to prepare. However, they're preparing because they have to, which usually motivates the least possible amount of preparation.

There are less punitive approaches to quizzing, which can result in more and deeper engagement with the content. Quiz questions that test conceptual understanding, not knowledge of facts and bits of information, help with retention and much research supports the value of regular review for increased understanding. Quizzes do take time to prepare. If you're new to teaching, you can start incrementally with a few quizzes, adding more every time you teach the course. Quizzes also take time to grade. Online quiz mechanisms expedite that task. If you have students complete the quiz before class, and you have the results while you're preparing, you can address areas of misunderstanding and confusion revealed by the quiz results. The resource collection provided in this chapter identifies a number of creative approaches faculty are taking in their use of quizzes.

Testing practices that promote learning. For students, tests are often more about grades than learning. "What'd ya get?" they ask each other, not "What'd ya learn?" Grades are important, they matter, and there's no way around that fact, but we give students tests for two reasons. We have professional responsibilities to certify their mastery of material (that's the grade part), but we also give them because they promote learning. Students study for exams—well, most do—not always as much as they should, but by doing so they have encounters with the material. They review their notes, read the text, do sample problems, try to figure what they'll need to know—all activities that usually result in learning. This raises an important question for teachers: how do we maximize the learning potential in exams? The research suggests we can do that with review sessions, exam alternatives, and debrief sessions. The resources here also recommend using cumulative quizzes, tests, and finals, even though they are terribly unpopular with students. It's important to remember that education shouldn't be about what students like, but about those policies and practices that promote learning. Cumulative testing and comprehensive finals are practices that do.

Reasons for extra credit, dropping low scores, or makeup exams. If you haven't already, you'll soon discover that students, sometimes even very conscientious ones, sometimes blow an exam or have an emergency that causes them to miss a testing event. First, you have ascertain whether the excuse is legitimate, and if so, decide what you will do about it. Dropping the lowest quiz score is a common practice among faculty who give quizzes. It's easy and takes care of the problems for most students. Make-ups are a lot of extra work for faculty—you have to create a whole new test and then arrange for the student to take it.

Students love extra credit, but most faculty don't offer it. They think it encourages students to put less effort into the big tests and assignments because they can do extra credit and make up for whatever they've missed. Poorly designed extra credit does look and feel like busy work, and if it is, then it's not very good at promoting learning. But that's not an inherent flaw with extra credit. If it's a well-designed, intellectually substantive assignment, it can be a second opportunity to learn important material, to learn material more deeply, or to learn entirely new material.

Preventing cheating or promoting academic integrity. Cheating is an endemic problem, with large percentages of students reporting that they and their peers engage in this behavior. Most faculty devote considerable time and effort trying to prevent it. Most spend much less time promoting academic integrity—trying to get students to understand that the person most hurt by the cheating is the person doing it. It's a hard sell, but worth trying, because what makes students who've gotten away with cheating in college think they can't get away with it in professional arenas?

Quizzes

Quizzes That Deepen Engagement with Course Content

by Maryellen Weimer

Reason to read: Here are seven creative approaches to quizzing—they're less punitive and more likely to promote engagement with the content.

I've been rethinking my views on quizzing. I'm still not in favor of quizzes that rely on low-level questions where the right answer is a memorized detail or quizzing strategies where the primary motivation is punitive, such as forcing regular reading of assigned material. That kind of quizzing doesn't motivate reading for the right reasons and it doesn't promote deep, lasting learning. But I keep discovering innovative ways faculty are using quizzes, and these practices rest on different premises. Here are seven examples.

Mix up the structure. Elizabeth Tropman makes a strong case for reading quizzes. She changes the quiz structure on a regular basis. Sometimes it's the usual objective questions, other times it's short-answer questions, or it might be a question that asks for an opinion response to the reading. Some quizzes are open-book; a few are take-home. This creates an interesting way to give students experience responding to different kinds of test questions and to keep quiz experiences from becoming stale.

Reference: Tropman, E., (2014). In defense of reading quizzes. *International Journal of Teaching and Learning in Higher Education*, 26(1), 140–146.

Collaborative quizzing. Lots of different options are being used in this realm. Students do the quiz, flip it over, and stand up to talk with a partner, to others in a small group, or with whomever they choose. After the discussion, they return to their quiz and may change any of their answers. Alternatively, students do the quiz individually, turn it in, and then do the same quiz in a small group. The two quiz scores are combined, with the individual score counting for 75 percent of the grade and the group quiz 25 percent (or some other weighted variation). Collaborative quizzing is an effective way to generate enthusiastic discussion of course content and reduce test anxiety.

Reference: Pandey, C., & Kapitanoff, S. (2011). The influence of anxiety and quality of interaction on collaborative test performance. *Active Learning in Higher Education,* 12(3), 163–174.

Quizzing with resources. Students take detailed notes on the reading because they're allowed to use those notes during the quiz. The same approach works with quizzes that cover content presented during class: students may use their class notes while taking the quizzes. The pay-off is a good (or better) set of notes for use during exam preparation. Ali Resaei reports that open-note quizzing coupled with collaboration resulted in significantly higher final exam scores in his quantitative research methods course.

Reference: Rezaei, A. R., (2015). Frequent collaborative quiz taking and conceptual learning. *Active Learning in Higher Education,* 16(3), 187–196.

Quizzing after questioning. Before the quiz occurs, students are given the opportunity to ask questions about potential quiz content. The instructor and the class work on finding the right answer or discuss the merits of possible responses. If someone asks a question that stimulates a lot of good discussion, that question becomes the quiz question and students have the designated amount of time to write an answer. One professor offered a variation: if a variety of good questions have been asked, answered, and discussed by a variety of students, the professor may tell students they've just had their quiz and give everyone present full credit. This approach encourages students to ask better questions and facilitates substantive classroom discussions.

"Community Space" quiz support. Audrey Deterding came up with this alternative "to inspire the often dull quiz routine." (p. 3) At the beginning of the class, two randomly selected students have three minutes to write anything the wish from the assigned materials on the board, which become a "community space." Students may use anything that's been written there during the quiz as a resource. The two students may collaborate with each other during the three minutes; the rest of the class remains silent. A student selected to write may decline, but a replacement will not be chosen. According to Deterding, "The expectation that [students] may have to share information in the community space motivates most students to closely read the assigned materials. They want to help their classmates perform well on the quizzes and they don't want to appear lazy or irresponsible to their peers." (p. 3) Deterding also reports that the approach encourages collaborative learning and creates a sense of community in the class.

Reference: Deterding, A. L., (2010). A new kind of "space" for quizzes. *The Teaching Professor,* November, 3.

Online quizzes completed before class. Students complete an online quiz before class. The quizzes are graded electronically, with a compiled summary going to the professor so there's enough time to look at the most frequently missed problems and/or identify areas of misunderstanding. Class time can then be used to address those concepts that are giving students the most trouble.

A way to make up a missed question. It's the standard daily quiz format: three conceptual questions answered during the first five minutes of class. No make-ups are allowed, but the three lowest scores are dropped and one missed quiz question per day can be made up by voluntarily participating during class discussions. This is one of several motivational features of this quiz design.

Reference: Braun, K. W. and Sellers, R. D., (2012). Using a "daily motivational quiz" to increase student preparation, attendance, and participation. *Issues in Accounting Education,* 27(1), 267–279.

The advantage of regular quizzes is that they provide ongoing opportunities for retrieval practice, and much cognitive psychology research (like that summarized in the reference below) documents the benefits of frequent testing. Regular quizzing does improve class attendance and gets more students coming to class better prepared. Those are not trivial benefits, but with a few different design features, quizzes can also promote deeper engagement with the content, further the development of important learning skills, and provide teachers and students with feedback that promotes learning.

Reference: Brame, C. J., & Biel, R., (2015). Test-enhanced learning: The potential for testing to promote greater learning in undergraduate science courses. *Cell Biology Education—Life Sciences Education,* 14 (Summer), 1–12.

Expanded version of a Teaching Professor blog post, March 30, 2016

Exams and finals

Test Review Sessions: A Better Design

Reason to read: Do you need to be persuaded that time in the course should be devoted to review before the exam? Would you be interested in a review session design where students are working harder than the teacher? They are, after all, the ones who need to review.

Terence Favero begins where many teachers are with respect to review sessions. Students request them. Teachers don't like to give up class time to essentially go over material they've already covered. It's difficult find a time that works for everyone—students don't want to come in early and professors don't want to review at bedtime. Then there's the issue of who shows up for the review session. Usually it's not the students who most need to be there. And finally, there's how review sessions are generally structured. Students ask questions, which the professor answers, while the students take notes. Favero notes, "Rarely does this approach lead to deep learning or prepare students for an exam." (p. 247)

With all this in mind, Favero decided to redesign his review sessions. He decided to hold them during a regularly scheduled class session. On the syllabus, he lists them as "review" or "test preparation" and has nearly perfect attendance that day in class. "Like many teachers, I came to the conclusion that if I wanted my students to become problem-solvers, I had to provide them with low-stakes opportunities and time to solve them." (p. 248)

Next, he changed the focus of the session from a rehash of content to solving problems. Says Favero, "Because of the vast amount of information contained in textbooks and electronic media, most students today have a difficult time discerning the essential content of the discipline and how it might be used to solve problems." (p. 247) To help students develop better problem-solving skills, Favero has used two different active learning strategies. The first he calls an "open-ended strategy." Students start by writing down the five most important facts, theories, or concepts from that section of the course. They partner and compare lists. Favero then tallies and lists the topics on an overhead transparency. He adds topics which students may have missed and then arranges the list in order of importance, discussing with students why these are the topics they should be reviewing for the exam. Next, students work in groups to generate two or three multiple-choice questions for each topic on the list. These are presented and answered collectively in class. "Students regularly question each other on confusing language or selection of the answers, again revealing what students know (or don't) and how they know it. Time permitting, we rewrite the questions so they could be exam-worthy." (pp. 247–248)

Favero also uses a second strategy he describes as "closed-ended." He brings to class eight to ten questions taken from previous exams. "I typically avoid knowledge or comprehension questions and focus on application-, analysis-, and synthesis-type questions." (p. 248) All the questions involve problems, and Favero works hard to get students to outline key concepts and pieces of the problem first. "I try to get students to hold off selecting the answer. Too often, I find that student learning short-circuits when they attempt to identify the answer without first identifying how to solve the problem." (p. 248) He always includes a "tricky," as in difficult, question in this group—not to frighten students, but to talk them through how challenging problems can be approached. "Explaining challenging questions before an exam gives students a better chance of learning how to problem-solve before they are in the middle of a stressful exam." (p. 248) This strategy also does an excellent job of removing hidden agendas. There are few surprises on the exam itself. Students correctly anticipate the kind of problems they will be asked to solve.

Students don't always embrace these review structures when they first experience them. They are used to asking questions and getting answers, and these sessions require them to work! This process also effectively reveals to students whether or not they are prepared for the exam. Favero notes that even though the sessions initially cause frustration for students, in the end, they do reduce pretest anxiety.

Finally, he notes with some surprise that these review activities have revealed strengths and weaknesses in his teaching. Sometimes he thinks material presented on a particular topic has been well explained and is understood by students. The review sessions may reveal that students either didn't understand at all or are holding misconceptions. "The review sessions help me identify content areas that need attention, something that end-of-semester evaluations do not." (p. 248)

Reference: Favero, T. G. (2011). Active review sessions can advance student learning. *Advances in Physiology Education,* 35(3), 247–248.

Reprinted from *The Teaching Professor,* Jan 2012

Short addendum: A faculty member (I'll call him Sam) who read Favero's article came up with an interesting version of one of his strategies. Sam starts with the question students most want answered during a review session: "What's going to be on the exam?" He tells students what most of them already know: the vast majority of teachers are going to do their best to not answer that question. "It's a question students need to be able to answer for themselves."

So Sam challenges students to quickly look over the material in their notes and the text that will be covered in this exam, then to write down five things they are pretty darn sure they will need to know for the exam. He gives them three to five minutes to complete this scan and review. Next, he tells them to share their lists with two, three, or four students sitting nearby; they should come up with seven things everyone in the group agrees they will need to know. Those items are written down and given to the instructor.

Without commentary, Sam integrates the lists and posts a class list on the course website. "Here's what your classmates think you'll need to know for the exam." The payoff comes during the exam debrief, when this class list appear as a PowerPoint slide. The class then marks off items on the list that did, in fact, end up on the exam. Sam says it's usually close to 80 percent, and what wasn't on the student list makes for good discussion.

How does Sam know the strategy is a success? Students regularly ask if they can compile a list during the next exam review session.

Note: It's a good ideas to have the exam prepared before reviewing student lists so as not to be influenced by their lists.

Cumulative Exams

Reason to read: Here's an example of the evidence that supports the value of cumulative exams.

Students don't like cumulative tests—that almost goes without saying. They prefer unit exams that only include material covered since the previous exam. And they'd like it even better if the final wasn't a comprehensive exam, but one last unit test. But students don't always prefer what research shows promotes learning and long-term retention, and that is the case with this study of the effects of cumulative exams in an introductory psychology course.

The study examines exam performance of students in two sections of the course. In the noncumulative course, students took three 50-question multiple-choice exams and a comprehensive final in which 55 percent of the questions covered material from across the course. In the cumulative course, students took three 50-question multiple-choice exams, but the second and third exams both included 10 questions covering material from the previous exams. Students in this section took the same final as those in the noncumulative section. Additionally, students in both sections took a follow-up exam two months after the course ended. That exam included 50 multiple-choice questions covering course content, which were not questions that appeared on the exams taken during the course.

Students were also surveyed about their exam preparation, studying, and preferences. As predicted, those taking the noncumulative section were happier with the exam format than those in the cumulative section. Other than that, there were no significant differences in the students' perceptions of things like exam difficulty, their study methods, or the number of hours they reported they spent studying for the exams.

But there *were* differences in students' performance on the final, on chapter quizzes, and in their overall course grade. All these differences favored students in the section with cumulative exams.

The researcher also divided students in each section into low- and high-scoring groups based on the scores earned in the first exam. (College GPA could not be used to group the students, as most of them were first-semester college students.) These groupings revealed some of the most interesting findings from this study. For students in the high-scoring group, quiz grades were unaffected by section, but students in the low-scoring group of the cumulative section did better on the quizzes than low-scoring students in the noncumulative section. This difference was statistically and academically significant. Low-scoring students in the cumulative section averaged a B quiz grade, whereas those in the noncumulative section averaged a C quiz grade. The same effect was seen in final course grades, with those in the cumulative section ending up with a B average and those in the noncumulative section with a C+ average. This pattern emerged again in scores on the exam taken two months after the course ended. High-scoring students' long-term retention was not affected by the experimental manipulation, but low-scoring students remembered more if they had the cumulative exams.

The researcher explains the results this way: "Most likely, having multiple cumulative exams motivates low-scoring students to engage in behaviors that promote better performance and long-term retention. High-scoring students probably already have the motivation to engage in these types of behaviors." (p. 18)

Is it worth risking student disfavor by giving cumulative exams? If those exams promote long-term retention (and this isn't the only research supporting that finding), it's a worthwhile risk. Students can be told about this research, content covered previously can be regularly mentioned in light of current content, and teachers (or high-scoring students) can work with students on those study strategies that effectively prepare them for cumulative questions.

Reference: Lawrence, N. K. (2013). Cumulative exams in the introductory psychology course. *Teaching Psychology,* 40(1), 15–19.

Reprinted from *The Teaching Professor,* Feb 2013

Helping Students Prepare for Cumulative Exams

Reason to read: There are some pretty simple, straightforward ways faculty can help students prepare for cumulative exams.

There are several reasons why students don't like cumulative exams and finals. First, they're more work. Rather than four weeks' worth of material, students must know and remember an ever-growing body of content. However, the research strongly supports that continued interaction with the content increases the chances that it will be remembered and can be used subsequently. One of the reasons students don't like cumulative exams is that most of them don't know or don't use study strategies that promote content retention. They wait until just before the exam and then start reviewing. Here are some ways teachers can help student develop and use study strategies that make preparing for and doing well on cumulative exams easier.

- **In comments,** the teacher explains the educational rationale behind cumulative finals. They are not being used because the teacher enjoys making courses hard for students. They are being given because research has shown that students remember course content longer and are better able to apply what they have learned. Moreover, the teacher is committed to helping students prepare for those exams throughout the course. And the teacher is open to student suggestions: what could done in class, outside of class, or online that would help students effectively prepare for the cumulative exams?
- **In class,** when new content relies on or relates to previous material, pause and let students recall or find that previous content. Where is it in their notes? In the text? How does knowing this previous material making understanding the new content easier? Obviously, this takes time, and

teachers may not be able to be this deliberate in each class session, but they can say there's a connection that students should be looking for when they study.

- **At the beginning of class,** quickly put students in small groups. Give them five (maybe more, maybe less) questions drawn from previous content. Let them find the answers. The first group to get all five answered correctly gets bonus points, treats, stars or pats on the back. They get more of the reward if they can also correctly say or list where the answer can be found.
- **At the end of class,** during those five minutes of summary time devoted to highlighting the day's content, take a few more minutes to tie in previous content; if a summary really isn't needed, take the time to have students review notes taken on a previous day. "Everyone take a couple of minutes and look at your notes for October 23. What are the key ideas you have in your notes?" "What do you have about X in your notes?"
- **Instead of a quiz,** students should prepare a potential exam question on material covered during the last two weeks. Their questions are submitted before class (in lieu of a quiz) and if the teacher finds five potential exam questions, those are posted on the course website. For the five posted questions, the author of each gets a bonus point.

    There are lots of variations here. Students can be given the option of submitting potential exam questions at any time during the course. If any of those questions end up on an exam, the student author should get the question correct and possibly get a bonus point.

    There is merit in having students write potential exam questions. It's a good review strategy and it gets them thinking about questions, not just trying to memorize answers. They don't write good test questions automatically, which means some resources might need to be made available online and samples of good and not so good questions might need to be discussed in class.
- **On quizzes and exams,** include a designated number of items that ask about content from previous units. To reinforce the importance of these questions, maybe they are worth an extra point or if a student gets them all correct, he or she gets some amount of bonus credit.
- **In study groups** which the teacher can encourage students to form, the group could be given a chunk of content and tasked with preparing a study guide (including study questions) on the material. These study guides could be distributed to other students in the class. This could be a course assignment or an extra credit option.

Revised version of a piece published in *The Teaching Professor*, Aug/Sep 2013

Recommended Resources: Three innovative exam formats

Bassett, H. M., (2016). Teaching critical thinking without (much) writing. Multi-choice and metacognition. *Teaching Theology & Religion*, 19(1), 20–40.

— After answering each multiple-choice question, student provide a short written rationale for their answer, which is graded along with the answer.

Corrigan, H. & Cracium, G., (2013). Asking the right questions: Using student-written exams as an innovative approach to learning and evaluation. *Marketing Education Review*, 23(1), 31-13.

— Students write and answer their own test questions; they're graded on the content and difficulty of their questions.

Knierim, K., Turner, H., & Davis, R. K., (2015). Two-state exams improve student learning in an introductory geoscience course: Logistics, attendance, and grades. *Journal of Geoscience Education*, 63(2), 157–164.

— Students complete exams in two stages: first, they do a typical closed-book exam on their own; then they do an open-book or take-home exam, alone or in collaboration with others, depending on how the teacher designs this testing strategy. Usually the first stage score counts more than the second stage.

Final Fitness and the Louisiana 2-Step

by Tena Long Golding, Southeastern Louisiana University

Reason to read: Most of the time, students don't get feedback on their final exam beyond the score. Here's a creative approach that gets them plenty of excellent feedback.

It has always bothered me, as a student and now as a teacher, that students seldom get feedback on their final exam performance. In most college courses, the final is scheduled after classes have ended, so there is no "next" class to return the exam and discuss the results. Posting exam solutions on the course website may interest some students, but most just scan for answers rather than analyzing the solution process and comparing it to their own. More often than not, a student only thinks about the final exam in terms of how it affected his or her final grade.

I teach a mathematics content course for pre-service elementary teachers in which problem-solving and reflections are part of what I emphasize across the entire course. My overarching goal for these students is developing their mental "fitness" to solve problems. I struggle with how to use every exam experience to both assess and expand my students' problem-solving abilities. I also want them to reflect on their exam performance. The Louisiana 2-Step, a state fitness initiative to promote the overall health of its citizens, sparked an idea as to how I might better use the final to improve the math fitness of my students.

I redesigned my final exam in this class so that it required two steps: a student step and a teacher step. The student step was the traditional "you take the test." Students spent the first part of the exam time responding to the problems. Since this was a mathematics problem-solving course, there were no short answer questions. All problems required a multi-step process.

After completing the exam, students traded their lead pencils for colored pencils and the key to the exam, both of which were used in Step Two.

The teacher step was a self-assessment component (SAC) which allowed students to evaluate their solutions from the teacher's perspective. Students were instructed to assess each question and their answer based on the key provided. Most of the problems could be worked in more than one way, but the key offered only one method. Students were reminded that their solution strategies could differ from the key, but the answers should be the same. In some cases, this allowed students to see an alternative solution process, while for others, it provided reinforcement of their chosen strategy.

Students were allowed to award points for their solution strategies and answers. In every case, they were required to make comments that explained and justified the points awarded, even if they got the solution "right." This enhanced their communication skills and provided the opportunity to examine and expand their own thinking as they compared solutions and evaluated the worth of minor or major mistakes and misconceptions.

The final exam was submitted to me after the completion of both steps. Although students did not know their exact score when they left (I still needed to grade the exams), they did have a good idea of their results. More importantly for me, students had a chance to analyze their solutions and reflect on their problem-solving strategies.

As this 2-Step final was a new idea, I used a short web-based survey to assess my students' views of its worth and to provide another opportunity for reflection: theirs and mine. On the e-mail survey, sent out immediately following the exam, students were asked to indicate their level of agreement—strongly agree, agree, strongly disagree, disagree—with the following items: 1) The self-assessment component (SAC) provided immediate feedback for my performance; 2) The SAC enhanced my problem-solving abilities by requiring me to reflect on my solution processes; 3) I learned more by completing the SAC; and 4) The SAC was a valuable activity. The survey was completed by 80 percent of the class, with 100 percent responding with Strongly Agree or Agree to all the items. There was also a section available for student comments. One student wrote, "It helped me see what I got wrong and the reason why I got it wrong. It helped a bunch and I think you should do it for your classes next semester." Another added, "It is a great way to assist in understanding the problems."

The final exam often carries the most weight and takes the most time (study time and test-taking time for the student; prep time and grading time for the teacher), but students reflect least about this cumulative course experience, which can be instrumental in integrating content across the course. Including a self-assessment component in my 2-Step final exam provided my students with immediate feedback on their solutions, enhanced their problem-solving skills as they examined and compared solution processes, and ensured they spent time reflecting on their performance on the final and in the course.

Reprinted from *The Teaching Professor,* Aug/Sep 2010

Reasons for extra credit, dropping low scores, or makeup exams

Make-Up Exams

Reason to read: If you're interested how other teachers handle make-up exams and why students miss exams (including more evidence that they make up excuses), this research offers a good overview.

They're a hassle. Depending on whether it means constructing a different exam, arranging a time and location to administer the exam, or grading after the fact, make-up exams can consume a lot of extra time and effort. Unfortunately, they are pretty much a necessity. Most of our institutions require faculty to excuse students for certain events and activities, like a serious illness, court appearances, military duty, and university-sponsored athletics.

Finding a lack of literature on the topic, two faculty researchers in marketing decided to seek answers to several interesting questions, starting with how make-up exams are typically handled by faculty. To answer that question, they collected 146 syllabi from 57 faculty members. Almost 87 percent of those syllabi listed some sort of make-up policy for assignments, primarily exams. Nearly 77 percent of faculty required students to contact them in advance to indicate that they would be missing the exam, 76 percent required written documentation for excuses, and almost 79 percent only let students miss exams for university-stipulated reasons. Less than 30 percent indicated the period within which the make-up needed to be completed and about the same percent specified a day of the week for make-up exams, with some seeking to deter their use by scheduling the exams early Friday morning or late Friday afternoon.

Also of interest is how often students missed exams. Here the researchers looked at several semesters of a large course with four exams and a final. During one semester, the miss rate was 3.34 percent and the second semester it was 2.37 percent. Almost all the absences involved medical reasons, with a few for deaths in the family, out of town interviews, and court appearances. The most often missed test was the fourth exam and the least often missed was the final. With tongues slightly in cheek, the authors write, "Interestingly, we observed a situation where relatively large numbers of students were sick, grieving, or taking job interviews at the time of the fourth exam. However, the following week, there were no make-up finals because the class was apparently filled with healthy students who postponed job interviews and were not grieving the loss of a loved one." (p.110)

Most faculty have questioned the legitimacy of a student-offered excuse and most have these suspicions more or less regularly. The authors note that "for unethical students, make-up exams represent an opportunity to cheat." (p. 105) They may discuss the exam with other students, not letting on that they have not yet taken the exam, or they may skip the exam debrief session but ask peers specifically about test questions and answers; if it's a very large class, they may even attend the debrief hoping they won't be noticed.

The authors also reference other survey results in which 72 percent of the student sample surveyed indicated they had asked to be excused under false pretenses while in college. Thirty-five percent said they had used a fraudulent excuse this semester. In this cited survey, 62 percent of the students said that less than 25 percent of their professors required any kind of proof for excuses. Does this encourage students to fabricate excuses?

Faculty can end up expending a good deal of time and energy trying to separate legitimate excuses from those that are not. Some students make it easy by regularly asking for make-up exams and extended deadlines. Other times, it's not always easy to differentiate a real excuse from one that is fake. A good policy for missed exams needs to find a balance between making it so easy that students regularly miss exam dates and assignment deadlines and making it so draconian that those with legitimate reasons to miss are punished for circumstances beyond their control.

Reference: Abernethy, A. M., & Padgett, D. (2010). Grandma never dies during finals: A study of makeup exams. *Marketing Education Review,* 20(2), 103¬–113.

Reprinted from The Teaching Professor, Aug/Sep 2011

Recommended Reference

MacDermott, R. J. (2013). The impact of assessment policy on learning: Replacement exams or grade dropping. *Journal of Economic Education,* 44(4), 364–371.

This study looked at the effects of three alternatives on cumulative final exam scores in a microeconomics course: three exams, each worth 20 percent of the grade, and a cumulative final worth 40 percent of the grade; three exams, with the lowest score dropped (making each exam worth 30 percent of the grade) and the cumulative final counting for 40 percent; and three exams, each worth 20 percent, with a cumulative replacement exam, offered at the end of the course, that could be used to replace the lowest score on one of the three exams, plus the regular cumulative final worth 40 percent of the grade. The study took place across multiple sections of the course, all taught by the same instructor, with the content, instructional methods, and test types remaining the same.

The results are interesting. Dropping the lowest test score did not compromise performance on the cumulative final. "Contrary to previous research and conventional wisdom...allowing students to drop their lowest grade improved performance on a cumulative final exam, while offering a replacement test had no significant effects." (p. 364)

Revisiting Extra Credit Policies

by Maryellen Weimer

Reason to read: Whether a course should include extra credit opportunities depends. Here's some of what it depends on.

I remember being surprised when I first read the results of a survey on extra credit published some years ago in *Teaching of Psychology*. Almost 20 percent of the 145 faculty (across disciplines) reported that they never offered extra credit, and another 50 percent said they offered it only under exceptional circumstances. The two most common reasons for not giving extra credit were that it encouraged lax, irresponsible student attitudes and that it was unfair to offer such opportunities to select students (say, those doing poorly). I also think extra credit is avoided because it means more work for faculty and most of us already have more of that than we can handle.

The question of giving students an extra chance is, like most pedagogical issues, less cut and dried than it might first seem. If the second chance is designed so that it represents a robust learning opportunity, if its completion means that a student who hasn't mastered the material finally does, and if learning is our ultimate goal, then complete opposition to second chances or extra credit seems less defensible.

We also should be called to take a second look by some of the creatively designed strategies teachers use to give students a second chance. They are far removed from the ubiquitous worksheet that can be dashed off with little cerebral effort. For example, I recently re-read an article I haven't read for some time and had forgotten that it contained what the author calls a "second-chance exam."

Here's how it works. The instructor attaches a blank piece of paper to the back of every exam. Students may write on that sheet any exam questions they couldn't answer or weren't sure they answered correctly. Students then take this piece of paper with them and look up the correct answers. They can use any resource at their disposal short of asking the instructor. At the start of the next class session, they turn in their set of corrected answers, which the instructor re-attaches to their original exam. Both sets of answers are graded. If students missed the question on the exam but answered it correctly on the attached sheet, half the credit lost for the wrong answer is recovered.

The benefits of this strategy? Students reported that they thought they learned more from having to look up answers rather than just being told the answers during the debrief. They also reported that the strategy reduced exam-related stress. The teacher felt the strategy put students at a higher cognitive level. They had to think about the question, determine an answer, and then decide whether or not they had answered the question correctly.

Does a strategy like this contribute to lax student attitudes? They still suffer consequences if they don't know something. They have a fairly short timeframe to track down the correct answers. And it isn't a strategy offered to some students and not to others.

There is no question that students are hungry for extra credit. Often, they seem more motivated to do the extra credit than the original assignment. Is that because they think extra credit is easier? Or does the motivation derive from not having done as well as they expected on an assignment? It could be the latter. A few years back, someone wrote an article for The Teaching Professor which described a kind of "insurance policy" extra credit assignment. Completing sets of extra homework problems was optional, but if students turned them in on the designated date, points awarded for the problem sets could be applied to a subsequent exam. Surprisingly, only a few students took advantage of this "insurance" option.

I'm left thinking that student attitudes about extra credit (which we probably have to admit derive from previous extra credit experiences) are not the best, and I'm not sure we help them learn when we succumb to what they want. But I also believe there are some viable ways to offer students a second change and some legitimate reasons for doing so.

References:

Norcross, J. C., Harricks, L. J., & Stevenson, J. F. (1989). Of barfights and gadflies: Attitudes and practices concerning extra credit in college courses. *Teaching of Psychology,* 16(4), 199–203.

Deter, L. (2003). Incorporating student centered learning techniques into an introductory plant identification course. *NACTA Journal,* June, 47–52.

Reprinted from The Teaching Professor blog, July 20, 2011

Prevent cheating or promote academic integrity?

Cheating: Are We Part of the Problem?

by Philip Johnson, Pima Community College, Arizona, and University of Phoenix

Reason to read: A faculty member responds to the research reported above. There are instructional practices that make cheating irrelevant and academic integrity the norm.

I was saddened to read in the February issue of *The Teaching Professor* the article about widespread cheating in business schools, as reported in the *Journal of Marketing Education*. Saddened, not because of the prevalence of cheating, but because colleges and college teachers seem to have created such an adversarial relationship between themselves and their students. Grades seem to have taken precedence over learning. Indeed, ethical behavior and honesty are important issues, but perhaps it would be useful to look at ourselves, our courses, and our teaching methods, as well the ethical deficiencies of our students. Cheating can occur only if there is a zero-sum relationship between the student and the teacher. The teacher controls something that the student wants—a high grade—and can offer or withhold it, and in this dynamic, the competitive, adversarial relationship thrives. How can we establish a more cooperative relationship with students, so that they are not our competitors, and so that the emphasis moves toward learning rather than merely grades?

Cheating is an issue only in relation to grading, not to learning itself. If a student really wants to learn, cheating to get a better grade is not part of the equation. It detracts from the student's sense of responsibility for his or her own learning, and obviously gets in the way of real learning. Students often are so eager to get a good grade that all their efforts are focused on the grades, rather than learning itself.

Cheating is possible only at the lower levels of learning, such as simple recall of facts. Cheating is not possible when student work must demonstrate the analysis and synthesis of ideas. Most cheating would vaporize if we adopted integrative, student-oriented teaching methods, ones more appropriate than the simple transfer of information. Good teachers are more than experts, more than repositories and providers of factual information. Good teachers engage the student in the processes of learning, orchestrate the resources around the student, work with the student as a colleague in the learning process, and act as mentor and supporter, even friend.

In the most effective faculty support workshops I ever conducted, I asked teachers, in groups, to plan to teach a course in which they were not experts—management professors, for example, teaching a course in nursing; history professors teaching management; and mathematics professors teaching anthropology. In essence, I took away their content expertise and asked them to be only "teachers." They were upset, but the techniques they planned were wonderful—very student-centered and team-oriented, with the teacher as the students' colleague rather than expert; no lectures appeared. Together, the teacher and students sought resources and became a team in the learning process. In courses like this, cheating is all but impossible and the motivation to do so is also diminished.

I am not advocating that we teach content that we know nothing about, of course, but rather that we downplay our role as experts and help our students learn how to become their own learners.

Let me be specific and share approaches that diminish cheating and represent more integrative teaching.
- De-emphasize grades as much as possible. Involve students in the evaluation of their own learning. Emphasize objective, nonjudgmental feedback, teacher to student and student to student, rather than relying on grades and points to convey the most important part of the feedback message.
- Emphasize the teacher's role, in relation to the student, as colleague, coach, mentor, co-learner; one who orchestrates the resources rather than merely provides the information. Experts are a dime a dozen; good teachers are rare.

- Try to move beyond recall, thinking of the student as a sponge. As quickly as possible, get students into analysis and synthesis, implications and applications, developing generalizations, and theory building.
- Give take-home, open book exams. Encourage appropriate teamwork in learning. Use lots of small-group instruction, encouraging students to learn from each other and to cooperate rather than compete.
- Provide assignment options. Perhaps some students would learn more writing a journal than a paper, or could profit by planning and conducting independent research. If appropriate to your content, consider field trips that provide an experience which you and your students can then analyze.
- Help students to focus on their own learning. Ask often and sincerely, "How do you know that?" "How did you learn that?" "What is your experience with this concept?" Help students to become learners, not only learned.

Reprinted from *The Teaching Professor,* Apr 2005

Recommended Resource

Chapman, K. J., Davis, R., Toy, D., & Wright, L. (2004). Academic integrity in the business school environment: I'll get by with a little help from my friends. *Journal of Marketing Education, 26*(3), 236–249.

"Consistent with past research, our results indicate that most students will cheat at least some time during their academic tenure in college. Nearly 75 percent of all students will cheat at some point in some situation. Even more disconcerting is our finding that if we exclude those students who have admitted they cheated and those who say they would cheat in at least one of the [four] scenarios [used in this research], only 14 percent of the students are left." (p. 246)

Percentages being reported currently are not much different than these.

Something to think about...

"Cheating is not really considered a bad thing by students. Since everyone does it once in a while, it is kind of like going over the speed limit. Everyone knows that it is against the rules, but everyone still does it."

A male student made this comment in an exploratory discussion group used by the researchers referenced above to better understand students' beliefs and attitudes about cheating.

CHAPTER 7

•

Feedback and Grading

Introduction

Providing feedback and assigning grades are a big part of any teacher's job. They're big because in most courses they take a lot of time, and they're big because they're important. It's a good idea for teachers to head into these tasks having made some decisions about how they'll be approached.

Feedback expedites improvement; that's why students need it, but sometimes have a hard time accepting it. Most students, but especially beginning ones, are terribly connected to their work. A critical comment or a lower than expected grade is not seen as an assessment of what a student has produced or performed, but are viewed as judgments leveled against them as human beings. The feedback provided needs to help them gain the maturity necessary to see the work they've done and who they are as related but separate. It needs to be balanced feedback, identifying both positive and negative features. It needs to be offered constructively and with a focus on the future. What does the student need to do to take the skills demonstrated here to the next level? Find more suggestions about good teacher feedback in the resources that follow.

Teacher feedback is essential, but it's not the only source of input helpful to students. Students can learn from the responses of their peers. Many students feel uncomfortable in the peer reviewer role. They are worried about being critical of someone who, just like them, is a student and classmate. They question their expertise. But making the exchange of feedback a positive and useful process is a skill most students will need in professional contexts, and it's better to learn those skills now than later.

New research on feedback is starting to document that when students respond to the work of other students, the process provides them with important insights about their own work. They see how a confusing organizational structure inhibits understanding and start asking themselves about the structure they're using in their own papers. Self-assessment is another critical professional skill, and not one teachers spend much time developing.

As a result, students come to depend on feedback from others to judge their work. Input from others is necessary, but so is the ability to accurately assess the quality of what you've produced or performed.

One of the biggest challenges that teachers face with feedback is getting students to pay attention to it. The grade is what matters first and foremost. They may read the comments, but often the next assignment eloquently shows they didn't act on the feedback provided. The resources that follow offer some help with this problem, but getting students to understand that the feedback is just as important as the grade is a slow process, one that frequently leaves teachers frustrated and discouraged.

Grades matter, not just to students, but to their parents, to those who decide on scholarships, to interviewers, and to those in charge of admission to various professional programs and graduate school. You can't tell students that grades don't matter, but you do need to keep pointing out that they matter too much to everyone. When they matter as much as they do, grades frequently get in the way of learning. Unfortunately, it is still true that students can get the grades without much learning. Teachers can do something about that with careful course designs and continued emphasis on what students are learning, not what they're getting.

Most new teachers spend a lot of time grading. It can be a time-consuming, arduous task. It can be less so, but assigning grades fairly and providing constructive feedback is never a quick and easy process. Clear grading criteria expedite the process and make it more objective. Too much feedback can overload students; better to target feedback in those areas where it's most needed. And don't spend time correcting every error. Students are the ones who made the mistakes; they need to be the ones who learn how to identify and fix what they're doing wrong. If the teacher fixes everything, then how does the student learn?

Grading policies set many of the parameters for learning in a course. If an assignment counts for a significant portion of the course grade, then students who care about their course grade will spend a significant portion of their time on that assignment. If points are awarded for participation, that will motivate some students to participate. Teachers set course grading policies and decide how those policies will be implemented. Will the lowest quiz score be dropped? That's a teacher decision. Grading policies play a significant role in what students learn, how they learn it, and the conditions under which they learn.

Despite making efforts to grade fairly and objectively, don't imagine that students are always going to agree with the grades you assign. The "I didn't get the grade I deserve" conversation is one of the more challenging exchanges teachers have with students. Here again, some preparation can make the conversation more constructive, even though most of the time, students aren't going to be persuaded that they got the grade they deserved, even though they did.

Feedback from the teacher, peers, and self

Making Teacher Feedback Useful

Reason to read: Teachers can offer feedback that increases the likelihood that students will pay attention to it and act on it, and that kind of feedback isn't all that difficult to deliver.

It's not a new issue: why don't student use the feedback we provide to improve their performance (their writing, their exams, their professional skills)? A revisit is justified because it's such an important question and because answers are more elusive than we might expect. However, good resources can be helpful, and the one referenced here falls into that category.

As the author notes, "a vast number" of articles on feedback in educational contexts have been published. He aspired to do a comprehensive review of the literature, but as with so many educational topics today, that is all but impossible to do. His particular interest is "empirical research on students' use of feedback in higher education" (p. 65) and the feedback that teachers provide students. His review ends up considering 103 peer-reviewed studies published since 1990. The bulk of those studies focused on the feedback contained in comments on students' written work. Although there is great diversity in these studies and a plethora of individual findings, some contradictory, the author identifies five themes or "challenges" that emerge out of this collection of studies. They are explored in more detail in the article, which cites the various studies with relevant findings and challenges.

Feedback needs to be useful. Bottom line: students don't respond to feedback that they don't perceive as being useful. That includes short, one-word or short phrase comments and it includes those situations when there is no opportunity to act on the feedback. That's what typically happens when student submit papers at the end of a course. The course is over, there is no opportunity to use the feedback, and if that's the first feedback students have received from the teacher, providing it is pretty much a wasted effort.

Students prefer specific, detailed, and individualized feedback. When asked about their feedback preferences, students say they want a lot of feedback (19 studies are listed that identify this preference), but in studies that have analyzed their actual use of the feedback, "the length of the comments does not necessarily influence whether students address it." The problem here seems to be that students want feedback that tells them exactly when they need to do—they don't want to have to figure that out for themselves. Their assumption is that if they do exactly what the teacher says, then the changes they make will be positively reflected in a better grade. However, doing exactly what the teacher says does not necessarily promote learning. In fact, "there are indications that less-specific, detailed, and personal feedback, which requires the students to actively engage with the feedback...may be more productive to learning." (p. 68)

Authoritarian feedback is not productive. If teachers offer authoritarian advice, students will do what the teacher says and not learn much, if anything, from the feedback. So the better approach is to take "the part of a dialogue partner" who doesn't use imperatives, and who doesn't give primarily evaluative comments or deliver them in an insensitive tone. (p. 69) However, as long as the teacher is the one giving the grades, a significant amount of that teacher authority remains. Even if the teacher makes constructive suggestions, students are still motivated to try to figure out what the teacher wants and not see the larger implications of the feedback in terms of improved writing overall.

Students may lack strategies for the productive use of feedback. The question here is one of know-how. If students understand the feedback but still aren't able to fix the problem, then they don't use the feedback. According to the research cited, when students lack the strategies necessary to deal with the feedback, they respond with more diffuse strategies like saying they will "try harder" on their next paper, that they plan to "go over" their notes more often, or that they make a "mental note" not to use that phrase in their next essay. There is some promising research cited that when given explicit guidance on how to use feedback, students' revision skills improved.

Students may lack an understanding of academic terminology or jargon. Eleven studies are cited which document that "many students have problems understanding the meaning of the terms teachers use, or the criteria that teachers make reference to..." (p. 69) Model answers or exemplars given with the feedback help students with this problem, as do rubrics and the opportunity to talk about the feedback with the teacher.

Given limitations identified in the article, "a tentative conclusion from this review is that, in order to aid students in using feedback more productively, the transmission model of feedback, where the teacher passes on information to the student, needs to be replaced with a more active and dialogic model of feedback." (p. 72)

Reference: Jonsson, A. (2013). Facilitating productive use of feedback in higher education. *Active Learning in Higher Education*, 14(1), 63–76.

A revised version reprinted from *The Teaching Professor,* Jun/Jul 2013

Peer Review: Successful from the Start

by E. Shelley Reid, George Mason University, Virginia

Reason to read: Peer feedback is most commonly provided on written work. This author explains the value of peer feedback and offers suggestions that get students providing more helpful comments.

A year ago, I was sitting at a conference lunch table with nine other college and high school writing teachers when the discussion turned to peer review: students evaluating each other's essay drafts. I was surprised when one professor's comment, "I no longer assign peer review of student essays because the poor results aren't worth the class time it takes," was immediately assented to by six other people at the table. I asked the group what they meant by "poor results." Most of them agreed it was the quality of students' comments on each other's essays—at best vague and unhelpful, and often misleading or incorrect.

I understand that frustration, yet I have seen enough evidence, in composition scholarship and in my own classes, to be convinced that the whole process of peer review—from the first mention of it in a syllabus to the final use that students make of peers' comments—is a crucial part of learning to write better. Furthermore, I do believe that it's possible and important to help undergraduates learn to better read and respond to their peers' writing.

Faculty who evaluate peer-review sessions based on multiple criteria, not just the quality of student comments, can find themselves more satisfied with the process, more able to explain its value to students, and more interested in developing ways to incorporate it across the curriculum. In the sections below, I describe six benefits that peer review can bring to writing education, regardless of—or, one hopes, in addition to—the production of useful student commentary.

Three by getting ready. Merely by requiring a peer-review session, I can address three key learning goals before the class meeting even starts. First, by assigning a peer-review draft, I broaden the audience to whom student writers are responsible: students must at least consider that someone other than The Teacher will see their writing. Second, students are required to produce a draft earlier than they might otherwise have done. Third, I have indicated to students that I will (and therefore, that they should) value students' input as readers of each other's writing. Not all students will take these learning opportunities to heart: some may ignore the invitation to perform well for their peers; some may not revise their initial draft; some may continue to doubt the value of "average reader" responses. But many students will reap these benefits.

Two for showing up. Having begun to read other writers' drafts, students can benefit in two ways before they write a single comment. As they see what their peers have created in response to the assignment, they can boost their own confidence in having written fairly well and/or see options for writing differently, if not better. Moreover, in asking students to consider questions about a peer's essay, I reinforce the idea that writing is the result of the writer's choices—which can be controlled and modified—rather than the result of an inspired, immutable vision. Confidence, control, and the ability to envision changes are crucial qualities of all good writers. I reinforce these learning opportunities by asking students to write reflectively afterward to describe something they saw in a peer's draft that could help them in their own writing, as well as something they saw that they don't think would work in their essays.

One in checking the bottom line. Finally, I can use my peer-review guide to help students check each other's essays—and indirectly, but more reliably, their own—against my assignment criteria. Questions that ask students to label places where peer-authors include vivid sensory details, integrate quotations smoothly, address counterarguments, or write an engaging title to the essay, for instance, invariably prompt students to ask me, "Were we supposed to include quotations?" or "What do you mean, 'counterarguments'?" Students who engage in such an active review of the assignment expectations, especially after they have completed a draft, increase their awareness of writing as a negotiation between the intent of the writer and the needs of the audience.

At the end of even a very-first peer-review session, then, I know—without looking at students' comments—that I have helped many students make progress toward meeting important learning goals. I share this vision of peer review with my students as well, discussing what they may have gained from the experience whether or not the most visible outcome—peer commentary—meets their expectations. Thus, even when students aren't ready to produce insightful and constructive feedback, I believe teachers and students can find satisfaction in the time they invest in the review activity, as long as they keep in mind all the ways that peer review can be successful right from the start.

Reprinted from *The Teaching Professor*, Oct 2006

Recommended Resource

Sadler, D. R., (2010). Beyond feedback: Developing student capability in complex appraisal. *Assessment & Evaluation in Higher Education,* 35(5), 535–550.

Representative of the new thinking about feedback, Sadler challenges the assumption that providing detailed teacher feedback is the best way to improve student performance. Instead, he proposes "intensive use of purposeful peer assessment" (p. 548) that enables students to recognize and judge quality when they see it.

Developing Students' Self-Assessment Skills: Is It Possible?

Reason to read: Getting students thinking about and assessing their own work can often happen as part of regular assessment activities in the course.

Here's an interesting thought: as students complete their assignments, they are assessing their work—asking themselves if they have written enough, whether their solution is correct, or if they've used enough references, for example. They answer those questions, thereby giving themselves feedback. If students are already assessing their own work, why aren't we working to build those abilities?

To get students involved in self-assessment activities, here are "seven principles of good feedback practice" that can be used to facilitate self-assessment skill development. They describe teacher interventions in the assessment activities students already do with the goal of improving their quality.

- **Good feedback practice helps clarify what good performance is.** When teachers design assignments and other learning activities, they have goals they hope those assignments and activities will accomplish. But successful accomplishment depends on students setting goals for those assignments and activities that overlap with the teacher's goals. The recommendation is that teachers consider providing students with exemplars and let students apply criteria and standards to those samples. Doing so gives students practice in identifying good performance.
- **Good feedback practice facilitates the development of self-assessment (reflection) in learning.** Students need "opportunities to practice regulating aspects of their own learning." (p. 207) This includes

practice in developing assessment standards and criteria. When students look at their own work, they often don't use specific or appropriate criteria. Teachers can tell them what criteria they should use, but at some point, students need to be able to generate appropriate criteria on their own, and these authors argue that's a skill that develops with practice. Activities that can be used include letting students identify areas where they would like to receive feedback, identifying some of the strengths and weaknesses of their work before they hand it in, and reflecting on their progress across a course (or part of it).

- **Good feedback practice delivers high-quality information to students about their learning.** "Feedback from teachers is a source against which students can evaluate progress and check their own internal constructions of goals, criteria, and standards. Moreover, teachers are much more effective in identifying errors or misconceptions in students' work than are peers or the students themselves." (p. 208) Although this may sound like what teachers do now, there is a difference: the goal of teacher feedback here is to help "students troubleshoot their own performance and self-correct." (p. 208) The authors recommend providing feedback when students still have time to make changes, limiting the amount of feedback and prioritizing areas for improvement.

- **Good feedback practice encourages teacher and peer dialogue about learning.** Students will better be able to assess their own work if they have the opportunity to discuss feedback with the teacher. That's noble but difficult when one has many students, as most of us do. However, students can discuss feedback with peers, including discussion of what particular comments mean based on the criteria used to assess their work.

- **Good feedback practice encourages positive motivational beliefs and self-esteem.** Research cited in the article documents that motivation and self-esteem are enhanced in courses with many low-stakes assessment tasks and when feedback provides information about progress and achievement, rather than focusing just on success or failure or how students compare with each other.

- **Good feedback practice provides opportunities to close the gap between current and desired performance.** The point behind this principle is simple: the only way to tell if a student is learning from the feedback is to see improvement in his or her work. Students need to be able to use the feedback to close the gap between what they

are doing and what they should be doing. The authors are in favor of letting students resubmit work or providing feedback on work in progress. They also recommend having students develop action plans in which they identify where and how they will use the teacher's feedback.
- **Good feedback practice provides teachers with information that can be used to help shape the teaching.** If teachers are going to provide good feedback, they need data on how students are progressing—not just on the assigned work, but also on how their self-assessment skills are developing. There should be regular discussions with students, particularly about those areas students find difficult.

One thing missing from this otherwise fine article is any discussion of the pressure most students feel to get good grades and how that pressure compromises their willingness to talk openly with teachers about the quality of their work. Why would you want to point out a weakness to the person who's going to grade it? Students need to understand that it is in their best interests to be able to accurately judge the quality of their work before the teacher does. This is an important skill, useful in college but especially relevant in professional contexts where work is not graded but still counts a lot.

Reference: Nicol, D. J., & Macfarlane-Dick, D. (2006). Formative assessment and self-regulated learning: a model and seven principles of good feedback practice. *Studies in Higher Education,* 31(2), 199–218.

Reprinted from *The Teaching Professor,* Feb 2012

Making grading a manageable task

Grading Advice for When There's Lots to Grade and Not a Lot of Time

Reason to read: Every teacher grades; most spend a lot of time doing it. Here's advice that can help you manage the task, keep your perspective, and maintain the quality of assessments.

- Make the grading pace steady, not frenzied, even if the stack of papers is inches thick. Take breaks regularly, even if they are only short time-outs.
- Try using a rubric if you don't already. They help keep you objective and focused on the task, and they make your expectations clear to students.
- If you're offering handwritten feedback on papers, presentations, or projects, remember: if students can't read it, there's no reason to write it. Grab a paper from the finished stack, hand it to a passerby, and ask them to read the comments on the first page.
- Keep the big-picture perspective. Don't get mired in too many of the details. Focus on two or three important points and make those clearly and concisely.
- Balance the feedback. Find something positive to say even when most of the feedback deserves to be negative.
- Offer at least some future-focused feedback. The next time a student completes an assignment like this, what's one thing they should keep in mind?
- Despite the comments students may make, grades are not something teachers give but something students earn.
- Even so, grades are assessments of a performance, not of a person.

Students (and some of their parents) have a really hard time understanding that, but teachers (even tired ones) need to point out the difference.
- Although it is very important that teachers grade fairly and objectively, grades are still imprecise measures of learning, despite the fact that our point systems are elaborate and carefully calibrated. These systems may make grading look precise, but it is not.
- Do your very best with the grades. Be careful and thoughtful. Grades do matter, often more than they should. They get students interviews and into grad school. They build confidence and diminish it. But in the larger scheme of life, grades don't matter. How long has it been since someone asked you what your GPA was? In contrast, how long has it been since you made use of the skills and knowledge you learned in college?

Adapted from The Teaching Professor blog, December 15, 2009

Rubrics: Worth Using?

Reason to read: Many teachers are finding that rubrics save them time grading while clarifying expectations for students. Might they work for you?

The use of rubrics in higher education is comparatively recent. These grading aids, which communicate "expectations for an assignment by listing the criteria or what counts and describing levels of quality from excellent to poor" (p. 435), are being used to assess a variety of assignments such as literature reviews, reflective writings, bibliographies, oral presentations, critical thinking, portfolios, and projects. They are also being used across a range of disciplines by a small but growing number of faculty.

This background is provided in an excellent article which examines the "type and extent of empirical research on rubrics at the post-secondary level" and seeks "to stimulate research on rubric use in post-secondary teaching." (p. 437) A review of the literature on rubrics produced 20 articles analyzed in the article.

So far, rubrics in higher education are being used almost exclusively as grading tools, even though some educators, like these authors, see them as having formative potential. When they are given to students at the time an assignment is made, students can use them to better understand expectations for the assignment and then monitor and regulate their work. They also make the grading process more transparent. In fact, in one of the studies analyzed in the review one group of students was given the rubric after their work had been graded, while another group got the rubric at the time the assignment was made. Both groups wanted to use rubrics again, but the rubric was rated as useful by 88 percent of the students who got it when the assignment was made as compared with 10 percent who rated it useful when it was returned with their graded assignment.

According to the study authors, "One striking difference between students' and instructors' perceptions of rubric use is related to their perceptions of the purposes of rubrics. Students frequently referred to them as serving the purposes of learning and achievement, while instructors focused almost exclusively on the role of a rubric in quickly, objectively, and accurately assigning grades." (p. 439)

For teachers who might be considering adding rubrics or using them as something more than a time-saving grading mechanism, the key question is whether rubrics promote learning and achievement. The authors of this review found the evidence inconclusive. One study did find that involving students in developing and using rubrics prior to submitting an assignment was associated with improved academic performance, but another study found no differences in the quality of work done by students with and without rubrics.

Also missing from the research so far are answers to questions related to validity and reliability. Do rubrics measure what they purport to measure—the validity question? "A large majority of the studies reviewed did not describe the process of development of rubrics to establish their quality." (p. 445) A bit more work has been done on reliability, and it shows that with training, separate raters consistently give similar ratings to a piece of work when using the same rubric. However, the authors note that more work on rubric validity and reliability is needed.

So are rubrics worth using? Among practitioners, there is general agreement that rubrics do expedite the grading process and make it seem more objective and fair to students. Among students, there is agreement that rubrics clarify expectations and are especially useful when preparing assignments. The researchers recommend "educating instructors on the formative use of rubrics to promote learning by sharing or co-creating them with students in order to make the goals and qualities of an assignment transparent, and to have students use rubrics to guide peer and self-assessment and subsequent revision." (p. 444)

Reference: Reddy, Y. M., & Andrade, H. (2010). A review of rubric use in higher education. *Assessment & Evaluation in Higher Education,* 35(4), 435–448.

A revised version reprinted from *The Teaching Professor,* Jan 2012

Something to think about...

"I believe that the teacher's challenge in evaluating students is less to separate the gifted from the ordinary than to find the gifts of the ordinary. And I believe we must communicate our evaluations in a manner that helps students understand their competence, or lack thereof, without destroying their confidence.... At best, grades are imprecise measures even of academic achievement. They do not weigh the worth of a student as a person, now or in the future." (p. 118)

Reference: Christensen, C. R. (1991). Every student teaches and every teacher learns," in Christensen, C. R., Garvin, D. A. & Sweet, A., eds., *Education for Judgment: The Artistry of Discussion Leadership*. Boston, MA: Harvard Business School Press.

Grading policies and practices that make grades more about learning

Using Grading Policies to Promote Learning

by Maryellen Weimer

Reason to read: Because grades are so important to students, they become too important to teachers. We start emphasizing them more than learning and beyond their importance. Here's some practices that redress the imbalance and let grading be more about learning.

I just finished putting together some materials on grading policies for a series of Magna 20-Minute Mentor programs and I am left with several important take-aways on the powerful role of grading policies. I'm not talking here about the grades themselves, but instead the policies we choose as teachers.

We take our grading responsibilities seriously, although most of us wouldn't rank grading among our favorite teaching tasks. Grades matter pretty much across the board. Who doesn't think they're important? But our focus is on the grades, not the policies that govern what's graded, how much a certain activity counts, or the mechanisms used to calculate those grades.

When students talk about the grades we've "given" them, we are quick to point out that we don't "give" grades—students "earn" them. And that's correct. It's what the student does that determines the grade. But that statement sort of implies that we don't have much of a role in the process—that we're simply executing what the grading policy prescribes. We shouldn't let that response cloud our thinking. Who establishes the course grading policy? Who controls it? Who has the power to change it? It's these policy decisions that involve us up to our eyeballs in grading matters.

Humphreys and Pollio write of grading, "Nowhere is the power that resides in the hands of faculty so apparent, or so open to abuse." (p. 96) We all aspire to be fair and objective in our assessment of student work, but there's so much to grade. We grade when we're tired and when we know whose work we're evaluating, and we don't stop being human when we're grading. Good grading policies have features that promote the fair and objective assessment of student learning. The criteria that differentiate the grade levels should be clear and relevant to the goals we have set for that test or assignment. Whether it is checklists or rubrics, we need to use these criteria religiously in the grading process, and I think they're rightfully and profitably shared with students, ideally before they start work on an assignment rather than once their work has been graded.

I also hadn't thought very thoroughly about how grading policies affect learning. What counts (papers, quizzes, tests, projects, participation, attendance, etc.) and how much it counts directs what students do in a course. The more an assignment counts, the harder students work on it. Yes, I know, we all have students who don't work on the tests and assignments worth the most, but for those students who are trying to succeed in the course, what counts and how much it counts directs where they focus their efforts, and that, in large measure, determines both what and how they learn.

Can grading policies motivate learning? Too often, they motivate getting the grade, not necessarily achieving the learning. Diane Pike, a sociology professor, objects to our overly detailed point systems that place a value on even the smallest activities. That grading policy feature reinforces the notion that unless there are points in play, the activity isn't worth doing. Detailed point systems also encourage grade grubbing—students in relentless pursuit of every possible point.

We have professional responsibilities to certify the extent to which students have mastered content, but we also have students do assignments and take tests because those activities promote learning. Students work with the content to complete an assignment. They study the material to prepare for exams. And our grading policies set the parameters within which that learning occurs.

Are there grading policy features that promote learning? What about the chance to use teacher, and maybe peer, feedback to improve an assignment before it gets a final grade? Or extra credit possibilities that allow a student to dig deeper into an aspect of course content that seems interesting? Or credit for course engagement, as in regularly attending class and being prepared, actively participating in group activities, meeting deadlines, and listening attentively to others?

I'm just suggesting possibilities here, which is to say, I'm still exploring ways to craft grading policies that enhance the fair and objective assessment of student learning at the same time they motivate learning. It's good to regularly review grading policies, freshly appreciating their powerful role.

References:

Pollio, H. R., & Humphreys, W. L. (1988). Grading students, in J. H. McMillian, ed., *Assessing Student Learning. New Directions for Teaching and Learning*, no. 33. San Francisco: Jossey-Bass.

Pike, D. L. (2011). The tyranny of dead ideas in teaching and learning: Midwest Sociological Society Presidential Address 2010. *The Sociological Quarterly*, 52, 1–12.

Something to think about...

"Complex point matrices end up training students to focus on the wrong things.... Students sit and calculate what things are worth, which assignments really matter, and adjust their behavior to maximize their situation—all perfectly logical responses. That is what the structure produces. Quantifying assignments, docking points for lateness, and intricate point systems of 400 or 1,000 points that are spread across varying categories distract students from what should be motivating their learning." (p. 5)

Reference: Pike, D. L. (2011). The tyranny of dead ideas in teaching and learning: Midwest Sociological Society Presidential Address 2010. *The Sociological Quarterly*, 52, 1–12.

Recommended Reference

Dobrow, S. R., Smith, W. K., & Posner, M. A., (2011). Managing the grading paradox: Leveraging the power of choice in the classroom. *Academy of Management Learning & Education,* 10(2), 261–176.

In this study, students were given choice about the weight of several assignments. Being able to choose how much the assignments counted increased reported levels of interest in the course and added to students' motivation to take additional coursework in the area.

When the student objects to the grade

The "I Deserve a Better Grade on This" Conversation

Reason to read: "I don't deserve a C! I put hours into this assignment. I get a C in this course and my scholarship is gone!" It's not an easy conversation, but it's a necessary one.

It's a conversation most faculty would rather not have. The student is unhappy about a grade—on a paper, project, exam, or for some other course assignment. It's also a conversation most students would rather not have. In the study referenced below, only 16.8 percent of students who reported they had received a grade other than what they thought their work deserved actually went to see the professor to discuss the grade.

Even though faculty might not want to increase the number of grade conversations they have with students, there is an interesting question here. Why didn't more students come to talk about the grade they didn't think they deserved? Maybe they really didn't have a problem with the grade, but only wished they'd done better. That might be true for some students, but this study tested (and verified) two theoretical frameworks that identify some of what makes these conversations difficult for students. They need to persuade the teacher, who has complete control over the grade, to change his or her mind—the grade decision has already been made and most teachers feel some pressure to defend their decisions. And teachers also know how badly students want good grades, whether they deserve them or not.

According to the theories which this research attempted to test, students must also behave in a socially appropriate way or they risk jeopardizing their overall relationship with the teacher, which may influence the grades they receive on subsequent assignments. One would hope that experience and maturity would enable teachers to maintain their objectivity, but students are often personally vested in their grades and not always sophisticated communicators. They may be defensive or angry, and unfairly accuse the teacher. Most of us have had a few conversations like this, which is why most of us would rather not discuss contested grades with students.

But these exchanges can be moments of learning for students and teachers, and they need to be thought of in this way. Teachers need to begin by listening to the student's objections and concerns about the grade. If it's a case of "you don't understand how hard I worked on this paper," it's an opportunity to discuss how difficult it is for teachers to assess effort and how grades are more about performance than effort. It's also an opportunity to ascertain whether the student understands the feedback that has been provided. Can they read the teacher's comments? Do they understand how and why partial credit is awarded? If a problem is present throughout the paper, can they identify unmarked examples of it?

It's possible the grade should be changed. Teachers need to have these conversations recognizing that grading (especially when doing lots of it) is not an infallible process. It is probably best to let the student make the case for the change, ascertain whether the feedback provided is correctly understood, then defer the decision to on whether to change the grade until the work can be reviewed without the student sitting across the desk.

The learning potential of these conversations is also a function of how forward-looking they are. "So what have you learned from this experience that will help you with the next assignment?" "What are you going to work on?" Here, depending on the student, it might be wise for the teacher to provide some guidance. "Let me identify three things to work on. All three would significantly improve the quality of your work, and if there is improvement in these areas, that will definitely be reflected in your grade."

If the student has conducted him or herself appropriately in the conversation, that deserves a comment. "I appreciate the maturity you've demonstrated in this conversation and although I'm sure you're disappointed that I haven't changed my mind about your grade on this paper, I do think these conversations are very important." And they are important. Teachers need to know when a student thinks a grade is unfair. They need to review their decision and they need to try to help the student understand why the grade stands.

How do teachers make it more likely that students will discuss concerns about grades and discuss them constructively? Teachers must talk more about the importance of these conversations. They invite students to come to the office to talk about grades they don't think they deserve. They explain why these conversations are challenging for students and teachers, and they give students good advice about what to say and not say about the grade they want changed.

Whether you're the teacher or the student, these aren't easy conversations. It's not in either party's interest to back down. But that need to defend a position should not become an obstacle that compromises what both parties can learn from these conversations.

Reference: Henningsen, M. L. M., Valde, K. S., Russell, G. A., & Russell, G. R. (2011). Student-faculty interactions about disappointing grades: Application of the Goals—Plans—Actions Model and the Theory of Planned Behavior. *Communication Education,* 60(2), 174–190.

Reprinted from *The Teaching Professor,* Feb 2012

CHAPTER 8

•

Feedback for Teachers

Introduction

Virtually all colleges and universities provide teachers with feedback via some sort of course evaluation system. Typically, it's student ratings, usually collected online at the end of the course. The same instrument is generally used in every course and the questions tend to be global ones, such as "How does this course/instructor compare with other college courses you've taken?" Those are what's called summative questions—they provide summary data. It's the kind of information institutions use to make personnel decisions. It's not information that provides teachers with the descriptive details they need to understand student experiences in their courses. It's important to participate in the end-of-course ratings process—sometimes jobs depend on it, and the results may prove motivating. But knowing that you do or don't compare well with other teachers does not reveal what you need to know to make informed decisions about changes.

Formative feedback can provide that level of descriptive detail. This is feedback the teacher controls, deciding who and what to ask. Resources here focus on three sources of formative feedback: **what I can learn about my teaching, what I can learn from students, and what I can learn from others.**

Most teachers make lots of judgments about their teaching, from what happened during a particular activity, to how it went in class today, and to conclusions about how the course went overall. Sometimes those judgments are made on the spot and colored with emotions. Conclusions are more objective if they're made after the fact and if they've involved some scholarly reflection. The biggest problem with instructor assessments is that what's concluded is often never submitted for verification.

Those in the best position to offer feedback as to how things are going are the students, who don't experience happenings in the course in the same way as the instructor. The biggest question to avoid asking students is whether or not they "liked" something. Education is not about what students like, but about those policies, practices, and behaviors the teacher is using to promote learning. That's what teachers need to ask about. And if students are invited to offer input, they can also be included in the discussion of what the teacher might do about the results. That doesn't mean the teacher must do whatever students suggest. For instance, there may be perfectly justifiable reasons to continue using essay exams even if students object. What the teacher could profitably do is explain the educational rationale behind the decision to continue and explore possible activities to help students better prepare for these kinds of exams.

All teachers, but especially those less experienced, can also learn a great deal about teaching from others—others who've written articles and books, others with particular areas of instructional expertise, others who've taught these kinds of students this kind of content and others who are recognized as excellent teachers. Much about teaching and learning can be learned from and with others. Let these resources be your introduction.

What can I learn about my teaching?

Writing to Reflect and Improve

Reason to read: Writing is a good way to slow down one's thinking about teaching. It also provides a record that can subsequently be reviewed and analyzed.

I grow ever more convinced of the power of writing to improve instructional practice. The process of putting ideas, feelings, and reactions into words slows the mind and permanently captures the thoughts. Even though these thoughts maybe be imprecise, or even inaccurate, writing puts them in a place where they can be looked at, analyzed more completely, and refined further.

The daily grind of teaching affords few opportunities for reflection; there's preparation for class tomorrow, there's papers stacked and waiting to grade, there's the student standing patiently outside the office door. But writing, specifically journal writing, can be accomplished quickly and with devices always at the ready; even five minutes allows enough time to record a range of thoughts.

Josh and Steve Boyd advocate the use of teaching journals, pointing out how college faculty commonly learn to teach by osmosis and self-education. They see journals a way for busy faculty to complement that process. In their work, they suggest three different types of teaching journals.

Descriptive journals. Some have called this kind of journal a "textbook of emergent practice." (p. 111) In its most straightforward form, it's simply of record of material covered in class. Boyd and Boyd recommend making the record more useful by including descriptions of student reactions. Did they get involved in the exercise? Did they understand the illustration? In their experience, these authors report having learned the most from their records of actual student comments: in answer to questions, when students took a different perspective, and when they provided direct feedback about a classroom event.

Comparative journals. "The comparative dimension of journaling goes beyond simply writing down what happens in class to examining the class from different perspectives." (p. 111) A bit later, the authors elaborate and offer an example. "Journaling provides an opportunity to recall which areas students had difficulty understanding and consequently, which areas we need to emphasize or explain more in the future. Comparing our instruction with the misunderstandings that might have resulted enables us to consider student perspectives; bad test questions (and why they were confusing or misleading), for instance, also find a place in the journal so that future exams will be better." It isn't always a record of what didn't work; journals work just as well to track where the teaching and learning connected and make suppositions about what precipitated that joining.

Critical journals. Critical here does not just mean critique, as in negative self-appraisal. Critical also means being reflective, considering broader implications and deeper meanings (p. 112). These journals take the teacher and the teaching to task in positive, constructive ways. Often the best time for critique (in both senses) is not at the point of writing, but after some time has elapsed and there is space for reflection, perhaps during the summer.

I first started journaling when teaching a new course. I felt unprepared and needed an efficient way of recording what else I needed to find and develop for the course. My quick notes helped greatly the next time I taught the course, but to my surprise, it was other comments, reactions, and feelings that caused me to reflect and approach my teaching more thoughtfully. In the beginning, I used to journal still thinking about audience: what if somebody else read this stuff? One of my English colleagues told me to see myself as the audience. This was writing for me. She recommended throwing journal writing away once read as a way to convince myself that there was no other intended audience.

If you haven't ever tried journaling about teaching, consider it a way of learning more about yourself as a teacher. You can approach the task very open-enddedly. Back in your office after class, write for five minutes about what happened. Let yourself write whatever comes to you. Don't re-read, edit, or revise, and don't read what you've written. After the course is over, read the journal from start to finish. I think you'll be surprised how much you learn.

Reference: Boyd, J., & Boyd, S. (2005). Reflect and improve: Instructional development through a teaching journal. *College Teaching,* 53(3), 110–114.

A revised version reprinted from *The Teaching Professor,* Dec 2005

Can You Write Your Way to Better Teaching?

Reason to read: Two faculty members from very different disciplines explore the benefits of writing about teaching.

Can you write your way to better teaching? Sociologist David Purcell thinks he did. He shares his method and what he learned from it in a detailed article. Purcell writes for 10 to 15 minutes after every class. If he teaches back-to-back sections, he makes comments on his lecture notes, which he uses to write fuller notes later in the day. He started doing this when he was a teaching assistant and continued the practice as a new faculty member. Using an autoethnographic analysis (a qualitative research approach), his conclusions about the value of this systematic approach are based on 43,000 words of notes from 14 courses written over a four-and-a-half-year period. The individual entries themselves vary from 125 words (when things in class went well) to 400 or 500 words (when things were in need of revision).

Purcell believes the writing these notes resulted in teaching improvements in three areas. "First, I have become a more confident, skilled teacher through this practice. I have improved specific aspects of lectures and class assignments, refined my course preparations, and polished certain techniques." (p. 13) Often, impressions about a class session are intuitive, based on feelings or a general sense of what happened. Writing gives those feelings substance. It identifies things a teacher can do something about. And if there are notes from several different times the class has been taught, there is a record not only of what needed to be improved, but of how it was changed and, as Purcell notes, that increased "my sense of mastery as a teacher." (p. 14)

Second, this systematic writing about course events expedites course preparation activities. "Daily preparation also becomes more efficient because you have a record of how successful that particular day was the last time you taught it, as well as any specific revisions you wished to make." (p.14) Even though the same course may be taught regularly, lots of time and other activities intervene between one semester and the next. And this time lapse is even greater if the course is taught less frequently. How nice to open a file of material and find a set of notes that suggest where you might most profitably focus your course preparation time.

And finally, Purcell believes that this regular reflective writing helped him grow as a sociologist. "Habitually viewing my teaching activities through a variety of sociological perspectives [described in the article] facilitates my use of the classroom as a key site for engaging in praxis." (p. 15)

Reference: Purcell, D. (2013). Sociology, teaching, and reflective practice: Using writing to improve. *Teaching Sociology,* 41(1), 5¬–19.

An abbreviated version reprinted from *The Teaching Professor,* Mar 2013

Matthew Liberatore explains in Chemical Engineering Education that a laboratory notebook holds an invaluable collection of procedures, measurements, calculations, and ideas on work undertaken in the lab. He thinks classrooms are a lot like labs and that teachers would benefit from a teaching laboratory notebook.

Isn't this what a teacher's lectures are? Liberatore doesn't think so. "[Lecture] notes are generally static and commonly show their age (wrinkled edges, yellowing paper, coffee stains, etc.)." (p. 271) He recommends something else: "I feel my courses have improved every semester by implementing a simple reflective exercise immediately after each class that I lead (even before checking messages)." He writes about what happened in class for just 1 to 2 minutes. Here's a list of the kind of things he might write about:

- What worked and what could be improved
- How long it took to cover each content segment
- Questions the students asked, especially those the teacher stumbled a bit to answer
- General energy level of the class and potential reasons for it
- Ideas for adding or subtracting content
- Ideas for starting the next class session
- Quiz or exam problem ideas

Liberatore offers this summary: "The teaching 'lab notebook' documents and organizes ideas, criticisms, and questions immediately following a classroom 'experiment,' and has led to improved organization and student learning of course concepts in the author's experience." (p. 271)

Reference: Liberatore, M. (2012). Two minutes of reflection improves teaching. *Chemical Engineering Education*, 46(4), 271.

Reprinted from *The Teaching Professor,* Apr 2013.

Something to think about...
"College teaching is the strangest of jobs. At the end of a class session, we may not know how it went, or we may think we know exactly how it went. Yet there remains the possibility to wildly misdiagnose the brainwave and heartbeat of that day's class." (p. 96)

Arvidson, E. S. (2008). *Teaching Nonmajors: Advice for Liberal Arts Professors.* Albany, NY: State University of New York Press.

What can I learn from students?

Negative Student Comments on Course Ratings

Reason to read: Most faculty have trouble dealing with negative student comments, especially when they seem so undeserved and off the mark. The underlying problem may not be the teacher's but the students'.

Most students don't arrive in our courses as sophisticated learners. They may not understand that learning is a process or may "have immature beliefs about how learning happens or how knowledge is created, not recognizing how tentative, iterative, and effortful a process it is." (p. 280) If that's the case, then student comments may actually reveal beliefs about learning that make their efforts to learn very challenging. To illustrate, the authors of one insightful article offer a sampling of common student comments made in three different kinds of courses.

Quantitative Classes
These are ones where students do lots of problem solving.
Student comment: "Problems on the exams were nothing like those covered in class or assigned in homework."
Most faculty find this comment especially irritating. Problems done in class are like those that end up on exams, and so students must not be paying attention, aren't spending time doing the problems, or just plain aren't studying enough. All of these things may be true, but it is also possible that "these student comments reflect the differences in the way novices approach problem-solving compared to experts." (p. 282) Students, as documented by other research, "rush to an answer, spending very little time thinking through various choices of procedure. They focus the importance of problem-solving on the answer rather than the process." (p. 282) Because

students are so answer-driven, they don't step back and see the overall structure of a problem—which is just like others done in class and on the homework.

How can teachers helps students develop this kind of insight? "Our problem-solving exercises for students must explicitly require them to spend meaningful time analyzing principles involved and envisioning how those same principles might be 'disguised' in other settings." (p. 282) This can also be accomplished by having students "annotate" their work on selected problems—that is, explain in writing what they are doing and why. The same insight can be achieved by having students explain to other students how they solved a problem.

Writing-intensive Courses

Student comment: "I don't understand the grading. We need to know what counts for points and what doesn't."

When writing papers, students often try to write what they think their teachers want to read. That's not entirely wrong—writers do need to write with their audience in mind. But students frequently translate this as conveying the "right" information—e.g., interpreting the poem the same way the teacher does—not as "the ability to construct an interesting, persuasive argument." (p. 283) Most writing assignments are designed to get students to produce information; students are far more comfortable reproducing information already received. So when they write a paper that says what their teacher has said and they don't do well, they are confused. They don't understand the grading criteria. One obvious solution is to have students openly discuss in class and with each other exactly what the writing task requires.

Students are also naïve about what the writing process entails. For them, the first draft is when the major time investment occurs. Editing is a simple matter of spellchecking and proofreading. Having students revise and rewrite—sometimes more than once—helps them see how ideas can grow and change as initial ideas are explored through writing.

Courses with Active Learning Formats

Student comment: "I didn't come to college to teach myself."

Students come to college already having lots of experience with teachers. They are used to teachers telling. They expect to learn from teachers, not from fellow students. When we observe students' feeble first attempts to figure things about for themselves, we are quickly convinced that telling is definitely the more efficient way. Indeed, "We...are frequently conditioned to think of teaching as telling, transferring our understanding and habits of mind by sheer force of will to our students." (p. 284)

It is always wise to share with students the educational rationale behind a decision to have them work out problems in groups, to generate examples with others, or to arrive at consensual decisions. The authors cast the problem and solution this way: "Too often we provide students with answers in our disciplines before they even understand the questions. Focusing more of our classes around the questions in our discipline and how we strive to find some answer to them can help students see the processes involved in the human quest for knowledge." (p. 285) Discussions like these move students beyond previous conceptions of teaching as information transfer.

The section on the course evaluation that asks for student comments is usually designed to provide insights as to how satisfied students were with a course. These authors wonder if that's what we really want to know. They suggest a variety of alternatives, such as asking students how their thinking about a subject may have changed or what the course has contributed to their development as thinkers or individuals. They recommend that we keep ourselves and our students focused on the kind and quality of learning experiences offered by and throughout the course.

Reference: Hodges, L. C., & Stanton, K. (2007). Translating comments on student evaluations into the language of learning. *Innovative Higher Education,* 31, 279–286.

Recommended Resource

Weimer, M. (2010). *Inspired College Teaching.* San Francisco: Jossey-Bass.

Chapter four (pp. 75–104) recommends a variety of instruments and activities faculty can use to solicit input from students with the potential to improve teaching and promote learning.

Sharing the Feedback

Reason to read: Feedback collection from students should be shared with them. Here's why.

In a study exploring what motivates students to provide faculty with feedback about teaching and learning, results indicated that students find it "desirable" when faculty share the results of the anonymous feedback they have provided the instructor. The author identifies five reasons why it's beneficial to share feedback results with students. I've added a couple more.

Sharing the feedback shows students that the teacher has looked at the results and is serious about using the feedback they've provided. It's a way of valuing student input, which can motivate them to provide more and better feedback.

Sharing the feedback gives teachers the opportunity to ask for clarification. This is especially valuable if results are contradictory or if it's not clear what actions in the classroom resulted in certain assessments.

Sharing feedback helps students put their assessments in context. Are their beliefs shared by the majority of students or held by only one or two students?

After sharing feedback, the instructor can propose possible changes and ask students for feedback on those before they are implemented.

Talking about the results gives the teacher an opportunity to explain why some recommended changes are not going to be made—e.g., what the students suggest would not allow the instructor to achieve important course goals, etc.

Talking about the results can provide an example of how feedback, even negative feedback, can be discussed constructively. It can model some of the principles of effective feedback.

Sharing gives teachers an opportunity to offer the class some feedback in turn. "You've given me some feedback about how my teaching is impacting your efforts to learn. I'd to give you some feedback on how your class is impacting my efforts to teach. I know I could teach better if you would give me more nonverbal feedback: look interested if you are; nod if you agree; smile if you hear something funny; look confused if you are. I promise I won't point out your confusion to the rest of the class. A lot of times, I look out and get no feedback. You look alive, but beyond that, I'm not seeing much response."

Reference: Caulfield, J. (2007). What motivates students to provide feedback to teachers about teaching and learning: An expectancy theory perspective. *International Journal for the Scholarship of Teaching and Learning,* 1(1), 1–13.

Revised from a Teaching Professor blog post, August 6, 2009

What can I learn from others?

Becoming a Better Teacher: Articles for New and Not-So-New Faculty

Reason to read: Faculty are readers. There just aren't a lot of norms expecting us to learn about teaching through regular reading. Lots of good scholarship on teaching and learning is embedded in our disciplines; even those the topics explored, activities proposed, and research reported have a much wider application. For examples that counter our beliefs about pedagogical reading, check out this reading list.

A couple of months ago, a colleague asked me to recommend a book for his new faculty reading group. I rattled off the names of several, but then wondered if a packet of articles might not be a better option. When I started to identify articles, it came to me that the what-to-read dilemma for new and not-so-new faculty goes beyond the articles themselves. It is more about the categories of work on teaching and learning rather than individual pieces.

Teaching and learning are multi-faceted phenomena—and that's how we should be thinking about them, right from the start. Books written for beginning teachers—in fact, lots of teaching books—focus on techniques. Yes, new (and experienced) teachers need techniques, but when that's the main focus, it tends to narrow the thinking and trivialize the complexities.

The literature on teaching and learning is diverse—one of its finest features, in my opinion. It can do a good job of shaping this broader thinking if it's sampled across disciplines, topics, and categories. I've been trying to come up with a set of categories—not one that captures all the kinds of scholarship, but rather one that is reflective of how those learning to teach (doesn't that include all of us?) ought to begin and proceed. So here's a set of categories to get us started and a few sample articles for each. I hope you will suggest other categories and examples that have helped you over the years, and feel encouraged to think about your pedagogical reading plans for the year ahead. How broadly have you been reading?

Learning to Teach at the Beginning and Beyond (with special respect for learning from mistakes)

More learning—possibly the most painful learning—happens early on (Collins), but learning to teach should be a career-long endeavor. Usually it involves change that grows out of new and evolving thinking about teaching and learning (Gonzalez).

Collins, H. (2009). On becoming a teacher. *The Teaching Professor* (May), 3.

Gonzalez, J. J. (2013). My journey with inquiry-based learning." *Journal on Excellence in College Teaching*, 24(2), 33¬–50.

Most of our students are dreadfully afraid of making mistakes. They fail to see the learning potential inherent in "error making." Are their teachers any different? If we want our students to learn from their mistakes, we ought to be learning from ours (Cohan and Delgado).

Cohan, M. (2009). Bad apple: The social production and subsequent reeducation of a bad teacher. *Change,* (November/December), 32–36.

Delgado, T. (2014). Metaphor for teaching: Good teaching is like good sex. *Teaching Theology & Religion,* 18(3), 224–232.

Challenging What's Accepted

We teach as we were taught, or as others in our department teach, or as those who taught the course before us did. Learning from others is great, but not if it is a passive acceptance that prevents us from challenging assumptions (Spence), questioning the unquestioned (Tanner), or pursuing the rationale on which a policy or practice rests (Singham). Reading in this category may or may not change our minds, but doing so challenges us to think and therein lies its value.

Singham, M. (2005). Moving away from the authoritarian classroom. *Change,* (May/June), 51–57.

Spence, L. D. (2001). The case against teaching. *Change*, (November/December), 11–19.

Tanner, K. D. (2011). Reconsidering "what works." *Cell Biology Education—Life Sciences Education,* 10 (Winter), 329–333.

The How-To, But with High Standards
Writing about teaching techniques has not always been robust. That's changed significantly in recent years, but it still feels as though there's not much new under the pedagogical sun. Teaching techniques tend to get passed around—used so often they become old hat, failing to inspire students or teachers. What's needed are truly innovative techniques, ones that turn teaching inside out.

Corrigan, H., & Craciun, G. (2013). Asking the right questions: Using student-written exams as an innovative approach to learning and evaluation." *Marketing Education Review*, 23(1), 31¬–35.

Hudd, S. S. (2003). Syllabus under construction: Involving students in the creation of class assignments. *Teaching Sociology*, 31(2), 195–202.

We also need in-depth explorations that help us raise regularly used parts of teaching to a whole new level of effectiveness. These focus on a small aspect of teaching (descriptions of writing assignments), tackle the how-tos of a common goal (teaching critical thinking), or parse the details of a multifaceted practice (grading). They're explorations that shine a bright light on current practice and how to make it better.

Van Gelder, T. (2005). Teaching critical thinking: Some lessons from cognitive science. *College Teaching*, 53(1), 41–46.

Rank, A., & Pool, H. (2014). Writing better writing assignments. *PS, Political Science and Politics*, 47(3), 675–681.

Schinske, J., & Tanner, K. (2014). Teaching more by grading less (or differently). *Cell Biology Education—Life Sciences Education*, 13 (Summer), 159–166.

Learning from Research
There's growing recognition that research findings can make teaching more evidence-based. But here's the problem: research is tough to read. These articles typically feature a detailed review of related research; a meaty section on methods; a discussion of results understandable only if you're fluent in statistics or qualitative methods; and a section on implications, usually for subsequent research, not practice. Teachers need scholarship that integrates (Michael and Prince) translates (Brame and Biel), and offers recommendations for practice (Dunlosky, et al.).

Brame, C. J., & Biel, R. (2015). Test-enhanced learning: The potential for testing to promote greater learning in undergraduate science courses. *Cell Biology Education—Life Sciences Education*, 14 (Summer), 1–12.

Dunlosky, J., Rawson, K. A., Marsh, E. J., Nathan, M. J., &

Willingham, D. T. (2013). Improving students' learning with effective learning techniques: Promising directions from cognitive and educational psychology. *Psychological Science in the Public Interest*, 14(1), 4–58.

Michael, J. (2006). Where's the evidence that active learning works? *Advances in Physiology Education*, 30, 159–167.

Prince, M. (2004). Does active learning work? A review of the research. *Journal of Engineering Education*, (July), 223–231.

Approaches That Promote Instructional Growth

In order to grow, one needs to know how—starting, I believe, with the personal narratives of others who have grown as educators. A well-written account of a teacher learning from his or her careful, critical analyses of teaching experiences can motivate a deeper level of personal reflection. But there are other approaches teachers have tried and found to be "growth promoting," such as learning about teaching by writing (Purcell) or growth prompted by "student" experiences (Gregory), or insights that come from our teaching stories (Shadiow).

Gregory, M. (2006). From Shakespeare on the page to Shakespeare on the stage: What I learned about teaching in acting class. *Pedagogy*, 6(2), 309–325.

Purcell, D. (2013). Sociology, teaching, and reflective practice: Using writing to improve. *Teaching Sociology*, 41(1), 5–19.

Shadiow, L. K. (2013). *What Our Stories Teach Us: A Guide to Critical Reflection for College Faculty*. San Francisco: Jossey-Bass.

Reprinted from the Teaching Professor blog, Jan 2016

What We Learn from Each Other

Reason to read: What we can learn from colleagues depends on what we discuss and who we have those discussions with.

When teachers tell me about some new strategy or approach they've implemented, I usually ask how they found out about it, and almost always get the same response: "Oh, a colleague told me about it." I continue to be amazed by the amount of pedagogical knowledge that is shared verbally (and electronically) between colleagues.

And I'm equally impressed by the spirit of sharing. Even if it's an idea I thought up myself, one I've spent time and energy developing, one I could ostensibly copyright or patent, if you want to use it—go right ahead. It's yours. There are no intellectual property rights on good teaching ideas, and that's a beautiful part of our culture.

Some new and impressive research verifies the strong role social interaction plays in our exchange of pedagogical knowledge. It's a study with a very specific context involving an elaborate interview design that collected data from 35 physics faculty members at a range of different institutions. They were asked about their understanding and use of Peer Instruction, capitalized because it refers not to generic student collaboration, but the protocol of individual answer, discussion, answer again developed in physics by Eric Mazur. Almost 60 percent of those interviewed said they first heard about Peer Instruction via an informal discussion with a colleague. Only 8 percent said they found out about it by reading. Higher percentages of those interviewed reported they learned more about the method through written materials, but the research team reports this conclusion: "Informal, social interactions among colleagues are a key mechanism of communication about reforms." (010110-14)

But there are some downsides to learning about teaching through conversations with colleagues, and this research highlights a significant one. The team identified nine features that characterize Mazur's brand of Peer Instruction and queried faculty about each of these. They discovered that almost half of their cohort who had been selected because they reported familiarity with Peer Instruction "did not indicate awareness of any specific features of PI [Peer Instruction] beyond getting students to work together." (101011-9)

When pedagogical innovations are passed from somebody who got the idea from somebody else, the fidelity of the information is bound to erode. The point isn't that faculty must use an instructional approach exactly as it was originally prescribed. We teach different content, different students, and in unique instructional settings. But as these researchers point out, when an instructional intervention such as Peer Instruction (or team-based learning, or cooperative learning or lots of others) has been studied and some of its essential features are subsequently modified or removed in practice, then what the research identified as results may not occur. It's now up to the teacher to ascertain whether the new form of the intervention is producing the desired effects.

Three final points: we can and do learn from each other, but when it comes to implementing something new, we should look beyond what we've heard about it from others. Fortunately, there's a treasure trove of information on almost every instructional intervention. It's fine to go ahead and adapt, to do what we think needs to be done to make the change work, but as the researchers discovered, the faculty in their cohort were making changes pretty much at random. True, there probably isn't going to be a readily available study that explores the changes exactly as you're proposing to make them, but there is likely more you can learn from others who implemented the innovation or those who've studied it.

We often get after our students who come to discussion without much background knowledge, related experience, or having done the reading. That lack of preparation affects the quality of the discussion. The same critique could be leveled against us. If all our pedagogical exchanges happen on the fly as we pass in the hall or pause in the mailroom, we're not having conversations that match the caliber of what we're trying to accomplish in the classroom. We can and should be learning more from each other.

And finally, we come to a point I've made previously: we need to choose pedagogical colleagues carefully. We select our research partners employing high standards. Pedagogical colleagues? Too often we share ideas and information with whomever happens to be nearby. All teachers are not equal when it comes to pedagogical wisdom. You will learn more from someone who knows more.

Reference: Dancy, M., Henderson, C., & Turpen, C., (2016). How faculty learning about and implement research-based instructional strategies: The case of Peer Instruction. *Physical Review Physics Education Research,* 12, 010110.

Reprinted from the Teaching Professor blog, April 20, 2016

• • •

Additional Resources
from Magna Publications

BULK PURCHASES

To purchase multiple print copies of this book, please visit: www.MagnaGroupBooks.com

MEMBERSHIPS/SUBSCRIPTIONS

Faculty Focus
www.facultyfocus.com
A free e-newsletter on effective teaching strategies for the college classroom.

The Teaching Professor Membership
www.TeachingProfessor.com
The Teaching Professor is an annual membership that reflects the changing needs of today's college faculty and the students they teach. This new fully online version of the newsletter that faculty have enjoyed for more than 30 years includes the best of the print version—great articles and practical, evidence-based insights—but also many new features including video, graphics, and links that make it an even more indispensable resource.

Academic Leader Membership
www.Academic-Leader.com
Academic Leader covers the trends, challenges, and best practices today's academic decision-makers. Members gain access to the latest thinking in academic leadership and learn how peers at other institutions are solving problems, managing change, and setting direction. New articles are published throughout the month.

CONFERENCES

The Teaching Professor Annual Conference
www.TeachingProfessorConference.com
This event provides an opportunity to learn effective pedagogical techniques, hear from leading teaching experts, and interact with colleagues committed to teaching and learning excellence. Join more than 1,000 educators from around the country.

Leadership in Higher Education Conference
www.AcademicLeadershipConference.com
The Leadership in Higher Education Conference provides higher-education leaders with an opportunity to expand leadership skills with proactive strategies, engaging networking, time-saving tips, and best practices. Attendees will hear from a roster of prestigious experts and nationally recognized thought leaders. A broad mix of plenary addresses, concurrent sessions, and timely roundtable discussions leave no topic untouched.

BOOKS

The Academic Leader's Handbook: A Resource Collection for College Administrators
https://www.amazon.com/dp/B0764KMC5Z
The Academic Leader's Handbook: A Resource Collection for College Administrators details an array of proven management strategies and will help further your achievements as a leader in higher education. Discover new leadership tools and insights at departmental, administrative, and executive levels.

Active Learning: A Practical Guide for College Faculty
https://www.amazon.com/dp/B071ZN8R32
Learn how to apply active learning methods in both small and large classes as well as in an online teaching environment. Whether you are new to active learning methods or experienced with them, this comprehensive reference book can guide you every step of the way.

The College Teacher's Handbook: A Resource Collection for New Faculty
https://www.amazon.com/dp/0912150688
The College Teacher's Handbook: A Resource Collection for New Faculty provides the essential tools and information that any new teacher in higher education needs to confidently lead a college classroom.

Essential Teaching Principles: A Resource Collection for Adjunct Faculty
https://www.amazon.com/dp/0912150246
This book provides a wealth of both research-driven and classroom-tested best practices to help adjuncts develop the knowledge and skills required to run a successful classroom. Compact and reader-friendly, this book is conveniently organized to serve as a ready reference whenever a new teaching challenge arises—whether it's refreshing older course design, overcoming a student's objection to a grade, or fine-tuning assessments.

Faculty Development: A Resource Collection for Academic Leaders
https://www.amazon.com/dp/0912150661
Discover proven tips and insights, from top academic experts, that will help you enhance faculty development programming and training on your campus.

Flipping the College Classroom: Practical Advice from Faculty
https://www.amazon.com/dp/B01N2GZ61O
This collection is a comprehensive guide to flipping no matter how much—or how little—experience you have with it. If you are just getting started, you will learn where and how to begin. If you have been at it for a while, you will find new ideas to try and solutions to common challenges. Flipping the College Classroom: Practical Advice from Faculty is an invaluable resource that covers all the necessary territory.

Grading Strategies for the Online College Classroom: A Collection of Articles for Faculty
https://www.amazon.com/dp/0912150564
Do your grading practices accurately reflect your online students' performance? Do your assessment and feedback methods inspire learning? Are you managing the time you spend on these things—or is the workload overwhelming? *Grading Strategies for the Online College Classroom: A Collection of Articles for Faculty* can help you master the techniques of effective online grading—while avoiding some of the more costly pitfalls.

Helping Students Learn: Resources, Tools, and Activities for College Educators
https://www.amazon.com/dp/0912150602
This collection is packed with ideas, strategies, resources, activities, assignments, handouts, and more for teachers to use in the classroom to help their students become better at the very thing they are there to do: Learn.

Features of the book include: summaries of current research (with full citations); assignments or quizzes to use in the classroom; handouts to distribute to students; review and reflection worksheets at the end of every section; and thoughts and reflections from Maryellen Weimer.

Managing Adjunct Faculty: A Resource Collection for Administrators
https://www.amazon.com/dp/B01N2OVK5W
Chances are your adjunct population has been built on an ad hoc basis to fill instructional needs. As a result, your institution might not have a solid management framework to support them. That's a gap you can close with guidance from *Managing Adjunct Faculty: A Resource Collection for Administrators*. This invaluable guide offers an extensive review of best practices for managing an adjunct cohort and integrating them more fully into your campus community.

Teaching Strategies for the Online College Classroom: A Collection of Faculty Articles
https://www.amazon.com/dp/0912150483
Includes online teaching strategies ranging from building a successful start of the semester, fostering productive connections, managing challenging behavior in the online classroom, and enhancing student engagement.

www.ingramcontent.com/pod-product-compliance
Lightning Source LLC
Chambersburg PA
CBHW060950230426
43665CB00015B/2143